THE
PLANT LOVER'S GUIDE
TO
FERNS

THE **PLANT LOVER'S GUIDE** TO

FERNS

RICHIE STEFFEN AND SUE OLSEN

TIMBER PRESS
PORTLAND · LONDON

CONTENTS

WHY WE LOVE FERNS

Ferns are an intriguing oddity of the gardening world, and their delicate beauty has inspired their use in gardens for generations. Their images permeate cultures through countless books, home décor, garden furnishings, fine art, tableware, and fabrics. Most amazingly, ferns surround and enchant us to such a high degree without the aid of a single bloom. When we turn to the garden, surprisingly many think of these incredible plants as a foil for others and as a secondary element in the landscape. Fortunately, some gardeners among us recognize the wealth of beauty these plants have to offer and the number of admirers grows by the day.

Why do we love these ancient leftovers from prehistoric times? Anyone who has walked through a fern-laden forest path can attest to the calming lushness ferns provide. As we observe this scenery, however, its simplicity disappears into an array of subtle details. With light passing through, fronds glow with a brilliant flash of green, new foliage unfurls to reveal more tones and colors unnoticed at first glance, and each frond is composed of a multitude of patterns. The depth of detail is complete with the revealing of dots, lines, and various patterns of sori on the underside of the leaf, whose purpose is to hold the fern's spores. The intricacies of sori can add color, texture, and just plain weirdness to these marvelous plants.

The new fronds of *Dryopteris erythrosora* (autumn fern) rival the color of any flower.

Their fantastic foliage is a compelling reason for using ferns in the garden. These plants can be the finishing detail of the shady landscape, perfect for softening edges and creating pleasing transitions between colors and coarse textures. Brilliantly colored new fronds and dramatically proportioned leaves can create an eye-catching delight. The ability of ferns to link and join plantings together effortlessly along with the endless variation and textural interest can feed even an obsessive collector's insatiable appetite.

Ferns have adapted to almost all climates and situations in gardens. Wild ferns can be found growing in marshes, rain forests or deserts, from valley floors to mountaintops, but our current cache of ferns has its main roots in Victorian England. Pteridomania, or fern fever, started in Britain in the mid 1800s and lasted until World War I. During this time amateur plant collectors and professional students of ferns scoured the countryside looking for rare species and any plant that deviated even by the smallest amount from the typical form. This enthusiasm for all things fern resulted in the selection and naming of hundreds of cultivars. Most of these selections were of ferns native to the British Isles and contained the beautiful, the unusual, the bizarre, and the ugly. Many of these forms no longer exist, but a surprising number have survived the test of time and are common in our gardens today.

Frost shimmers on the ruffled pinnae of *Polypodium cambricum* Pulcherrimum Group in winter.

Pteridomania led to the creation and perfecting of many ferny styles of gardening. Among the most popular garden features of the era were ferneries, specialized gardens for displaying ferns. Some ferneries were assembled in conservatories, with interiors sculptured with stone and concrete and lushly planted with ferns, while other structures were built in sheltered areas outside where cold-tolerant plants could be showcased. Protected outdoor areas were also developed into stumperies and rooteries. Weathered logs and well-worn root wads were gathered and sculpturally composed to create habitats for ferns and woodland treasures enjoying the cool moisture of the slowly deteriorating wood. Rock gardens with shady cool nooks were designed to help grow choice alpine and dwarf species difficult to cultivate in any other condition.

Although pteridomania began to fade after World War I, it did not vanish. Many of its horticultural oddities survived into modern times, but the fact is that we don't need these special garden features to grow ferns—just a patch of soil or lacking that a container for an apartment balcony.

In recent years, the global economy has opened the horticultural doors of the world, allowing botanists and researchers access to remote countries and regions. As a result, new species are being discovered and rare species rediscovered. Today's gardeners can enjoy a wealth of new ferns that has not been seen since the Victorian's golden age of exploration. It is a good time to be a gardener and a good time to grow ferns.

Ferns and other native plants at Moon Window, built of local stone, in the Caher Bridge Garden, County Clare, Ireland.

DESIGNING
WITH
FERNS

The superficial similarity in textures and forms of ferns can lead to a monotony that does not reflect the true value of these plants as ornamentals. In fact, ferns are some of the most diverse plants for the garden. The remarkable variation of foliage, size, and habit allows their use in a wide range of situations.

Beautiful gardens result not only from handsome plants but also from good design, and gardening with ferns is no exception. The principles of garden design are general rules that can help define an outdoor space as a cohesive garden, whereas design elements can be thought of as tools for defining the garden space and accomplishing the desired aesthetic goals.

Garden design should not be looked at as a rigid or difficult task. Attractive vignettes in the landscape can happen even if we don't consciously think about design elements and principles, but considering these design basics is a great way to start working ferns into the garden.

Cultivars of *Athyrium niponicum* are known for their colorful plumage.

Elements and Principles of Garden Design

The primary tools for defining garden space include color, line, shape and form, texture, and size. All of these elements are found in ferns, so putting ferns to good advantage in a garden simply involves following a few basic design principles, namely, balance, repetition, focal points, scale and proportion, transition, rhythm, and unity. Let's look at these elements and principles one by one.

COLOR

Color is the joy of the garden and one of the strongest elements in design. Good color decisions can make or break a planting. Although we commonly think of ferns only as green plants, they have an amazing diversity of color variations in the newly emerging fronds and in the hairy scales covering new growth. Some fronds even produce great autumn colors.

Fern fronds typically have one color playing off a green undertone. The common autumn fern, *Dryopteris erythrosora*, is a prime example. The new growth is a rich bronzered, especially when very young. As the frond matures, green becomes more prominent, until attaining a deep rich color. In truth, nearly every color can be seen on various ferns at some point in the year.

The intensity of frond color is often dictated by environmental and cultural conditions. For many ferns, growing them with less fertilizer and in leaner conditions often results in bright and more vibrant colors in new growth, but paler and smaller fronds at maturity. The more familiar you become with the plants, the more you can manipulate their environment to produce the effects you want.

LINE

Lines are the bones of the garden. They can be as literal as the edge of a driveway or a sidewalk or more subtle and implied. Tree canopies silhouetted against the sky or a meandering garden path are good examples. When we look at ferns, it is hard not to see the multitudes of lines each frond creates from its prominent stipe or midrib stem to the leaflets attached. The rigid lines of upright ferns reinforce a feeling of structure and stability, whereas the curved lines of arching ferns promote gentleness and relaxation.

Tones of bronze highlight the green in this *Blechnum* medley.

Ferns for Color

Adiantum hispidulum
Athyrium 'Branford
  Beauty'
Athyrium 'Ghost'
Athyrium niponicum
  'Pictum'
Athyrium otophorum
Blechnum chilense
Blechnum
  novae-zelandiae
Blechnum
  penna-marina

Dryopteris erythrosora
Dryopteris lepidopoda
Dryopteris wallichiana
Osmunda regalis
  'Purpurascens'
Woodwardia orientalis
  var. formosana
Woodwardia
  unigemmata
Woodwardia virginica

The sculptural curves of dried fertile fronds of *Matteuccia orientalis* add interest in the garden.

SHAPE AND FORM

Shape is commonly thought of in two dimensions, height and width, whereas form typically refers to three-dimensional objects. The terms are often used interchangeably in garden design along with the term *plant habit*. Shape provides a rather limited view of ferns. Form (or habit) is where this fascinating plant group excels. *Upright, mounding, weeping, spreading,* or *vase-like* are only a handful of the terms that can be used to describe fern forms. Good garden design starts with deciding what shape or form you want, and then finding a fern that will fit the bill, or, for the impulse buyer, finding a place appropriate for the form of a newly acquired plant.

TEXTURE

Texture, which is both tactile and visual, describes the roughness or smoothness of an object's surface. Ferns are champions in this regard. Every inch of these plants speaks of a lush foliage experience that can be enjoyed from a distance or down to the microscopic level. Typical terms like *coarse, medium,* or *fine* do not even scratch the surface of ferns. A textural vocabulary must be embraced to convey their variations and patterns fully.

SIZE

A wonderful quality of ferns is that they have a finite ultimate size. With the exception of tree ferns, they will not continue to grow taller once they are mature. This makes it much easier to imagine the space each fern will ultimately occupy, a very useful tool in designing a garden. Size is the tool we use to accomplish appropriate scale and proportion in the garden. Because ferns (with the exception of tree ferns) are generally small in comparison to many ornamental plants, they are useful for creating detail in smaller spaces. Larger spaces can be filled effectively by mass plantings and groupings.

BALANCE

The first principle of good design is balance. Balance refers to a visual equality when looking at an outdoor space. This equality can be accomplished by symmetrical or asymmetrical plantings. Formal gardens typically use symmetry to give a sense of order. Although ferns

The spiky fronds of *Asplenium scolopendrium* Fimbriata Group create an eye-catching form.

The large leaves of the tree fern *Dickso-nia antarctica* rise above the planting.

Leaves of *Asplenium scolopen-drium* Crispum Group have a delightfully wavy texture.

arc not often thought of as a component of formal gardens, they soften the harsher lines of formal plantings, while retaining a structural and uniform balance. A good example is two formal containers or urns placed on either side of an entrance of a finely clipped hedge path. Ferns with a strong vaselike habit work well in this role. Structurally interesting ferns like the evenly mounded *Polystichum polyblepharum* (tassel fern) or more upright and rigid *Osmunda regalis* (royal fern) could play a role in a formal setting.

The informal garden style common in today's landscapes often relies on asymmetrical balance in which different types of plants appear in various parts of the garden, but visually the amount of space taken up by plants in each part is about the same. Most ferns easily lend themselves to asymmetrical balance. Larger ferns can be used to offset the visual weight of smaller shrubs. Massed ferns can counterbalance larger shrubs and small trees, as well as add texture to the planting.

REPETITION

Repeated colors, textures, forms, or shapes link the garden together, giving it cohesiveness. Repetition can be accomplished by using the same plant throughout a space or by grouping matching plants in various locations. A multitude of fern species and cultivars are similar in texture or habit, and planting them as a grouping can satisfy a collector's lust for ferns while adhering to design principles. For example, a collection of *Cyrtomium* (holly ferns) can highlight the variation among species and cultivars, yet from a distance provide a sense of uniformity. Excessive repetition, however, can be monotonous and uninteresting.

FOCAL POINTS

Focal points are essential for leading the eye to areas of interest. Strong garden elements like patios, garden art, or garden furniture are natural focal points. Plants with extreme textural differences from their surroundings make excellent choices as well. Focal points are not only a single bold and interesting feature at the end of a trail, they also involve interesting groupings and clever use of texture. Straight lines and bold features speed the eyes' movement, whereas curves and soft or fine texture slow the pace through a space.

Larger more architectural ferns make a bold statement. The strong upright vase shape of *Dryopteris* ×*complexa* Stableri Group creates a compelling draw. The furry rough trunks of tree ferns such as *Cyathea cooperi*, along with the canopy of enormous fronds, scream for attention in mild regions, where gardeners are fortunate enough to grow them without protection.

Well-placed *Dryopteris* ×*complexa* pulls together the garden vignette.

Ferns with a Clumping Habit

Adiantum aleuticum
Adiantum pedatum
Athyrium otophorum
Dryopteris affinis
Dryopteris ×australis
Dryopteris ×complexa
Dryopteris erythrosora

Dryopteris filix-mas
Dryopteris intermedia
Polystichum munitum
Polystichum
   polyblepharum
Polystichum setiferum

Spreading Groundcover Ferns

Adiantum venustum
Blechnum chilense
Blechnum penna-marina
Dennstaedtia punctilobula
Gymnocarpium
   disjunctum
Gymnocarpium dryopteris

Matteuccia struthiopteris
Onoclea sensibilis
Phegopteris
   decursive-pinnata
Thelypteris kunthii
Woodwardia areolata

The repeated frond shape from more than one plant of *Polystichum neolobatum* (Asian saber fern) adds a sense of flow to the garden.

Ferns for Massing and Groundcover

MASSED AND GROUNDCOVER FERNS are great for creating repetition of texture, pattern, and form. Groundcover ferns are especially useful in the woodland. Their rambling nature allows them to find the most suitable location in which to thrive. Ferns for this purpose tend to have either a clumping to slow-spreading habit or a running habit characterized by vigorous underground rhizomes. The first decision for the gardener is to decide which of these two types would be best for a particular situation.

Clumping or slow-spreading ferns, such as *Dryopteris erythrosora* (autumn fern) and *Athyrium niponicum* 'Pictum' (Japanese painted fern), are best in a well-defined location. Due to their growth habit, clumping ferns tend to stay put and not crowd or shade out neighboring plantings. This growth habit is particularly beneficial for mass plantings that require ferns to be taller than knee height or where more than one type of fern is planted to create a tapestry of textures.

To achieve a full groundcover look, a good rule is to use the height of the fern to determine the spacing between plants. For example, ferns that grow 3 feet (1 m) tall should be planted at 3-foot (1-m) intervals. This spacing allows most ferns to grow together in about three to four years. Spacing can be reduced for a quicker fill. If you are planting more than one kind of clumping, slow-spreading fern in an area, allow more space around the tallest ferns, or the smaller fern's shape will be lost under the larger fronds.

Running, freely spreading ferns add a natural feel to the garden. They are useful in covering large areas and are excellent for providing a consistent texture throughout a planting. The rhizomes run around and through other plants, tying together a diversity of colors, forms, and textures. Using rambling ferns can be a freeing experience for the gardener, allowing these plants to decide where they want to be, and then editing other plants around them. Ramblers can also be a maintenance headache. Most spread by rhizomes, which are underground modified stems. Care must be given to provide adequate space and a containment barrier, or to plan regular removal of rhizomes that grow in unwanted places.

Short-creeping *Dryopteris erythrosora* (autumn fern) forms tight clumps of colorful foliage along a cliff face.

Both evergreen and deciduous ramblers are available, although in colder environments most suitable choices will be deciduous. Evergreen running ferns offer a consistent landscape component, generally only requiring trimming to the ground once a year to refresh the foliage. A beautiful and surprisingly tough evergreen groundcover is *Adiantum venustum* (Himalayan maidenhair), and a smaller and more slowly spreading choice is *Blechnum penna-marina* (little hard fern).

Deciduous spreaders offer a chance to create a multilayered landscape. Underplanting with bulbs—especially winter bulbs like hardy cyclamen or early spring ephemeral perennials—can build a richer and more interesting garden. *Gymnocarpium dryopteris* (oak fern) is a widely grown example, as well as the extremely vigorous *Dennstaedtia punctilobula* (hay scented fern). If a less-aggressive spreader is desired, try the frillier form of oak fern, *Gymnocarpium dryopteris* 'Plumosum'.

Fewer plants are required when planting runners in the garden. Space them at a distance three times their height. These ferns appreciate a well-prepared loose soil to spread quickly. Full coverage of an area will generally occur in two to three years, depending on the fern.

Deciduous *Gymnocarpium disjunctum* (western oak fern) will cover over *Anemone nemorosa* (wood anemone) as the latter becomes dormant in early summer.

The laciness of *Gymnocarpium dryopteris* 'Plumosum' makes it an attractive companion for *Blechnum spicant* and *B. penna-marina*.

Many ferns, however, slow the eye and lead to a more paced and reflective enjoyment of a garden. Arching fronds along a curved path reinforce each other, and the fine texture of many ferns invites a closer look. This is a great principle for encouraging the use of ferns with colorful foliage. The silvers, purples, and minty greens of *Athyrium niponicum* 'Pictum' are difficult not to notice and beg for closer inspection.

SCALE AND PROPORTION

When choosing ferns, it's important to achieve the right scale and proportion. Scale compares the size of one plant to that of another, whereas proportion refers to size in relation to all the plants in a given space. An easy way to think about the two concepts is to imagine a container of mixed plants. Scale allows us to see if one plant looks appropriate to the one beside it, but proportion allows us to look at the entire container to see if the sizes of all of the plants work well with each other. Ferns are plants generally of smaller size and typically have little impact on large spaces unless they are used in large numbers. However, they can add mass to a grouping to balance the planting and they can be used effectively in small spaces common in the urban landscape.

Wavy foliage and brilliant variegation make this selection of *Asplenium scolopendrium* hard to ignore.

A large fern in the distance leads the eye into the garden.

Attributes of Good Specimen Ferns

SPECIMEN FERNS RELY on exceptional foliage and form combined with a choice location to allow these traits to be fully enjoyed. A specimen fern does not need to be a large fern. Many medium and small ferns can serve effectively in this role.

Attributes of good specimen ferns include at least two of the following traits and preferably all three. First, the crown (the growing point or points at the base of the fern) should remain tight and compact. Loose, open, or slow-spreading clumping ferns rarely make a striking single specimen.

A tight crown generally contributes significantly to the second desirable trait, an even outline to the overall habit of the fern. Fronds emerging from the crown in evenly layered arrangements create a recognizable shape that, in combination with a repetitive pattern, is always visually pleasing. Specimen ferns benefit from a well-defined and familiar outline. Upright or broad vase-shaped patterns make a striking statement, but full mounded forms or long cascading fronds can also be attractive, and provide a sense of lushness and shapeliness.

Third, although perfect and shapely plants are classic for a good focal point, unusual cultivars can often make great specimen plants. Finely cut leaves, crested and frilly fronds, or weird and twisted growth can conspire to create a truly eye-catching plant. Specimen ferns are a welcome opportunity to expand your palette and try something new.

In this grouping of *Cyrtomium macrophyllum*, the differing frond sizes make the planting more interesting.

The arching fronds of *Dryopteris filix-mas* (male fern) soften and complement clipped hedges.

The rambling habits of *Gymnocarpium dryopteris* 'Plumosum' and *Blechnum penna-marina* establish rhythmic patterns in a woodland.

This large maidenhair fern (*Adiantum aleuticum*) smooths the transition from lower perennials to larger woody shrubs.

TRANSITION

Transition represents the gradual change from one space to another. It includes both horizontal changes on the ground level and vertical changes from ground level to the tree canopy. What we experience as we move through a garden is as important as the place toward which we are moving. Several means help to accomplish smooth transitions in the garden. Encouraging physical movement by walking is facilitated with paths, patios, open spaces, and garden features, but carefully placed plant material emphasizes and encourages this activity. The creative use of texture, color, and varying heights makes for an enjoyable transition. Take, for example, the finely textured soft-shield fern, *Polystichum setiferum* Divisilobum Group. By creating a hazy mass of fronds, this fern allows your eye to be drawn to bolder textures leading you to other areas in the garden.

RHYTHM

Rhythm completes the feeling of motion that leads you through the garden. It uses lines, colors, forms, and textures to weave plantings together and break monotony. Flowing arches of fern foliage reinforce the feeling of flow in a garden.

UNITY

When all of the landscape principles and elements work in agreement, the garden can be considered unified. Simply following good design principles will result in unity in the garden, but it is always wise to step back from time to time to look at the whole area and consider its development.

The common colors of *Cystopteris bulbifera* and *Rhododendron ochraceum* link these different plants together.

Ferns in the Formal Garden

Ferns add an air of elegance and soften the stiff strong lines associated with a formal style of gardening. Specimen ferns can be very effective in a formal garden, as the symmetry of the fronds and their repetitive and uniform patterns replicate the formality of the garden. Ferns are also perfect for containers or the classic urn, ready to be placed symmetrically in the garden.

Tightly clumping ferns are the easiest to work into a formal landscape. They stay in place, are slow to outgrow the location, and do not grow taller once they have reached their mature height. If a plant is lost, it is easy to replace, and the new fern will quickly fill in and match the existing ferns perfectly. Full mounded plants, such as *Polystichum polyblepharum* (tassel fern) or *Dryopteris crassirhizoma* (thick-stemmed wood fern), are excellent examples. These ferns can be used as a specimen or planted as an edge to a border or bed. If a taller fern is desired along a border, *D. filix-mas* (male fern) or *D. affinis* (golden-scaled male fern) are reliable choices. Very upright ferns add to the formal setting. The rigid narrow vase shape of *D. filix-mas* 'Barnesii' or the equally upright, but frilly *D. affinis* 'Cristata' look like marching soldiers in a row, with the narrow fronds of 'Barnesii' acting as the points of bayonets or, in the case of 'Cristata', looking like ostrich plumes on the soldiers' hats.

Ferns in the Woodland

With a large number of fern species growing naturally in forest conditions, it is no wonder they are a basic plant we turn to when gardening under trees. Most ferns thrive in shade and prefer humus-rich acidic soils. The kinds of trees that make up woodlands vary, but most forests can be categorized under two primary plant communities, deciduous or evergreen. These types of woodlands create very different conditions, which influence garden choices. Gardening under either type of tree offers unique challenges.

Because deciduous trees lose their leaves in autumn, deciduous woodlands are often brighter than their evergreen counterparts, with more light reaching the ground from autumn to late spring. Evergreen ferns provide winter interest here and ferns that emerge early in the season can take advantage of this extra light for robust growth. Even after the trees produce foliage, deciduous woodlands often allow more light through the canopy than evergreen woodlands with similar tree spacing. In addition, rain easily penetrates the canopy from autumn to spring, allowing soils to become more fully hydrated.

One advantage of deciduous trees is that their fallen leaves typically decompose readily and can be used as mulch. This decomposing layer helps retain moisture in the soil well into dry weather. Leaves that are slower to decompose, such as oak, can be shredded. Shredding foliage also provides a finer more finished appearance. In late autumn, care should be taken to uncover evergreen fern fronds to allow for photosynthesis through the winter months.

Evergreen forests include conifers such as pines (*Pinus*), spruces (*Picea*), and firs (*Abies*), as well as broad-leaf trees such as evergreen oaks (*Quercus ilex* and *Q. hemisphaerica*), southern beech (*Nothofagus*), and eucalyptus. Evergreen woodlands offer a dense overstory that helps hold warmer air closer to the ground in winter and defuse strong winds, creating microclimates that allow experimentation with marginally hardy species or ferns with a more fragile and delicate frond.

Shade is cast all year, making evergreen woodlands overall darker than their deciduous counterparts. Some pine forests are an exception to this rule, with widely spaced trees allowing for relatively bright open woodland conditions. Rain is slow to penetrate a dense evergreen canopy, and it may be necessary to water plantings regularly during dry weather or to limit your choices to drought-tolerant ferns. If extra watering is planned, make sure the existing trees will tolerate the additional moisture. Some evergreen tree species, especially from Mediterranean climates, require dry periods and do not tolerate summer watering.

Evergreen foliage, whether needles or leaves, tends to decompose more slowly than foliage from deciduous trees. Evergreen debris can make excellent mulch, with smaller leaves and needles being the best and easiest to incorporate into the garden. As an added benefit, decomposing needles leave an acidic residue that is preferred by most ferns. This

Ferns for Edging

Adiantum ×mairisii	*Polystichum aculeatum*
Blechnum spicant	*Polystichum ×dycei*
Cyrtomium fortunei	*Polystichum munitum*
Dryopteris cycadina	*Polystichum*
Dryopteris dilatata	*polyblepharum*
Dryopteris erythrosora	*Polystichum setiferum*
Dryopteris filix-mas	
Polystichum	
acrostichoides	

A woodland medley in the
garden of Ed and Kathy Fries
in Seattle, Washington.

slow-to-decompose mulch can form a thick layer and effectively deter weeds. Large foliage can be run through a shredder or lawn mower for a finer texture.

Woodlands are complex environments with intricate ecosystems above and below the ground. Successful plantings work within these ecosystems to enhance not only the beauty of the site, but also to encourage biodiversity of the living organisms that keep the woodland healthy. A primary goal of good woodland gardening is maintaining a thriving overstory. Trees are fierce competitors for water and nutrients and can have dense root systems that fill the ground beneath the canopy. A single tree can absorb thousands of gallons during the growing season, and during droughts leave little extra water for smaller neighbors. Most of the tree roots are in the upper 3 to 6 feet (0.9–1.8 m) of soil, with the majority of water- and nutrient-absorbing roots in the top 12 inches (30 cm). Most woodland gardens will experience dry periods during the growing season, so plan for this by planting ferns that tolerate dry conditions. A wide selection of ferns can thrive in this environment.

As massive and as permanent as tree roots may seem, trees are not indestructible. Care must be given to prevent severely damaging the root system during planting. To prevent extensive root damage, do not rototill under the canopy of a tree. Instead, work in smaller pockets of soil. Creating several small planting areas under the tree minimizes root damage. Sometimes cutting a root is inevitable. Try to leave roots that are over 2 inches (5 cm) in diameter when possible. It is best to allow 2 to 4 feet (0.6–1.2 m) between any planting and the trunk to give room for maintaining the plantings without damaging the trunk.

To ensure the health of woodland ferns, it is wise to have a long-term plan for managing the trees. Regular removal of dead or damaged branches along with a gentle thinning of the canopy allows light levels to be maintained below. To minimize damage to the fern plantings, carry out major pruning in autumn or winter. Summer is an excellent time to thin out the canopy, although all larger branches should be removed carefully to keep damage to the understory at a minimum. Anyone who has gardened under trees is familiar with the debris and litter that inevitably drop from above. Twigs and branches can be removed quickly and easily as part of a regular maintenance routine. Leaves, seeds, cones, and floral remnants can form part of an array of smaller debris that will drop to the ground throughout the season. Much of this smaller debris can be left where it has fallen to decompose in place.

The most successful woodland plantings take into account the available light, competition from other plants, soil conditions, and water provided during the growing season. Assessing a woodland area with these considerations in mind will not only guide

The remarkable red foliage of *Dryopteris erythrosora* (autumn fern) in spring. Once established in the garden, this species is drought tolerant.

the selection of ferns, but will also assist in placing them to their best advantage.

The textural quality of fronds is exquisite when sunlight is used to enhance the form. Through light and foliage, the fern structure can be enhanced, emboldened, or softened. Rays of sun streaking through the woodland can dramatically highlight emerald green fronds or add a sense of movement with dappled flickers reflecting from gently swaying foliage. The brilliant green from backlighting is most dramatic when light penetrates from low angles, whereas light coming from directly overhead often calms the woodland with a dappled glow.

Careful thinning of tree crowns or the selective removal of trees can transform dark underused woodlands into vibrant gardens. When pruning, think about what direction the light will come through the tree canopy at different times of the day and year, taking into account the times you are most likely to be in the garden. If you enjoy an evening stroll, prune so openings will allow the low rays of the evening sun to peak through. By thinning and raising lower branches along woodland edges and using larger specimen ferns along this edge, this dramatic backlighting can be best put to use. When opening the upper canopy, consider thinning branches on either side of a pathway rather than over the pathway. This will allow

The Fern Dell at the Dallas Arboretum

Fine-textured *Polystichum setiferum* Divisilobum Group under a birch tree.

A Cautionary Tale

PTERIDIUM (from the Greek *pteridion*, small wing) is the universally recognized bracken fern. In various manifestations, all of them extremely weedy, it is worldwide in distribution, and has the distinction of being the most widespread vascular plant. The rhizome creeps quite aggressively buried anywhere from several to 18 inches (45 cm) or more. The deciduous fronds are usually between 3 and 6 feet (0.9 and 1.8 m) tall, but can be taller. Blades are broadly triangular. Bracken fern is not here as a recommendation but rather as a warning, because it often shows up as an uninvited guest. Chemical sprays or diligent removal of emerging fronds eventually destroys the invasion. (At one time, it had many uses—all long gone—from thatching roofs to preventing flea infestations.)

With its long-creeping rhizomes, *Pteridium aquilinum* (bracken fern) can quickly cover a large area.

light into the surrounding beds and promote backlighting and a dappled effect when viewed from the path.

Backlighting ferns calls for plants with strong architectural form and interesting foliage. Large ferns or those with an upright habit are easiest to backlight well. Fine textures are highlighted when the sun streams through the frond, and this is a great way to show off crested and frilly cultivars or those with interesting coloration. Dappled lighting is excellent for groundcover ferns or those that are mass planted. Ferns with matte foliage show more texture with dappled light. Darker locations call for ferns with bold leaves, shiny fronds, or pale green foliage. Bold foliage draws the eye and adds textural interest in comparison with the surrounding plants. Shiny foliage reflects light and adds brightness to dark areas. Pale green fronds add a sense of freshness to dark locations.

Watering ferns is to be expected during the first few years of establishment. Depending on the ferns selected, additional watering may be necessary throughout their lives. It is important to make decisions about watering prior to planting. If the woodland will not be watered after the ferns are established, then the plant material should reflect this decision. It is easy to fall in love and plant ferns that don't entirely suit a completely drought-tolerant approach. Plan for plant lust, and set aside areas that are easily watered for those ferns that will need a little extra. Grouping ferns that have similar watering needs together makes sense both ecologically and financially.

Even with extra watering, locations with excessive root competition generally require drought-tolerant ferns. Ferns grow very slowly in dry locations and take up to five to seven years to reach maturity. Often these mature plants are smaller than the same fern grown in less competitive garden conditions. This slow development allows the fern to establish itself firmly and permanently. Try to plant in such competitive locations in autumn or early spring to allow the fern's roots to establish as much as possible before the growing season.

Most ferns are opportunists and fill a niche not taken by other plants in the ecosystem. Nearly every habitat has at least one native fern uniquely suited to its specific environment. Use natives as a backbone of woodland plantings through repetition or as groundcovers or massed groups to accentuate the regional character of the garden.

A stumpery made from log rounds in the Steffen/Peterson garden.

Most weedy ferns in the garden are well-adapted natives spreading into unwanted areas by underground runners or as overly abundant volunteers.

When selecting native ferns, avoid aggressive species unless there is ample space for them. Two excellent examples of vigorous-growing ferns are *Pteridium* species (bracken fern) and *Matteuccia struthiopteris* (ostrich fern), both native to vast areas, but each can engulf a garden if not given enough room to spread. Fortunately, there are plenty of well-behaved native species along with a rich diversity of well-behaved exotic ferns from around the world. Exotic ferns add interest, contrast with the native framework, and are essential to creating an interesting textural tapestry in the woodland.

STUMPERIES

The shaded groves of a woodland garden are an ideal location for stumperies, a nearly forgotten Victorian-era garden feature. Stumperies combined stumps, logs, and branches in an attractive arrangement much the way a rockery is created from stone. The earliest example of a stumpery is at Biddulph Grange in Staffordshire, England. Well-weathered stumps intertwine with contorted logs along pathways. Ferns and ivy dominate the garden, with pockets of moss and lichens filling the gaps.

Occasionally, stumperies are also referred to as rooteries or loggeries, depending on the primary material used. One of the best contemporary examples is the Hardy Fern Foundation stumpery in Federal Way, Washington, with several other excellent examples in public gardens in the United States and the United Kingdom to inspire gardeners.

Stumperies are not complicated to build and offer a unique way to display ferns and other woodland plants. They can be as small as a few stumps or logs in an urban garden. Although, nearly any wood can be used to create a stumpery, traditional ones rely on well-weathered old stumps from species of trees that have rot-resistant wood. The best stumps have interesting gnarled shapes with root stubs that have a unique fanged look.

Stumps can be cleaned with a pressure washer to remove any excess dirt and to reveal more character among the roots. Traditionally, the stump is placed upside down with the roots pointed up or on its side. To give a more natural look, the lower third of the stump can be buried in soil and compost. Logs and stumps can be stacked, but caution should be used to ensure they will not shift over time and fall. Less traditional stumperies combine many species of tree stumps together, with some rotting faster than others. The wood that is less rot resistant becomes the foundation for ferns that prefer to grow on trees and will serve as a nurse log for plants requiring moist, but well-drained positions.

Once the wood is in place, soil can be added. Most ferns thrive in a rich soil high in organic matter. Try to leave pockets between the stumps for plants to be added. The soil will settle over the next few months, and these holes and gaps can be filled as needed. Regular fertilizing will likely be required over the following few years, along with extra watering during dry periods.

Stumperies are not only great habitat for ferns, but also serve as habitat for local wildlife. The cool rotting wood is ideal for toads, salamanders, and newts. The abundance of vegetation and nooks formed by the roots provides nesting habitat for many birds. Fungi and mushrooms are another part of the stumpery ecosystem. Most fungi are not harmful to plants. If there is concern about existing disease problems on the site, use only rot-resistant species for the stumpery.

Ferns in the Rock Garden

Ferns may not be the first plant you think of for the rock garden, but there are several species of alpine and xeric (dryland) ferns that thrive in these conditions. There are also many dwarf and compact cultivars of common garden species that are easy to grow and widely available. If you are just starting to experiment with ferns in the rock garden, dwarf and compact cultivars are a great place to start. Many of these will grow in typical garden soils and do not require extra attention to their watering needs.

The rigid and upright *Dryopteris affinis* 'Crispa Gracilis' (dwarf golden-scaled male fern) and *Polystichum setiferum* 'Congestum Cristatum' (compact crested soft shield fern) are charming, tough, and evergreen and will tolerate some sun. One of the most delightful rock garden ferns is the deciduous *Adiantum aleuticum* 'Subpumilum' (dwarf western maidenhair). In bright light, it will only reach a few inches tall, with miniature palmlike fronds. For shady rockeries, try *Asplenium scolopendrium* Cristata Group (crested Hart's tongue fern) or the shiny-foliaged *Cyrtomium falcatum* 'Maritimum' (mini holly fern).

Weathered tree stumps create great habitat for ferns as well as other plants and wildlife.

One of the most delightful rock garden ferns, the deciduous *Adiantum aleuticum* 'Subpumilum' (dwarf western maidenhair).

True alpine ferns are the most challenging groups to grow, but one of the most rewarding when done successfully. A trip to the mountains will reveal a wealth of ferns thriving in thin rocky soil. These hardy plants are not typically found in the full blazing sun, but find their hold between the shelter of rocks and boulders or on the shady side of shrubs or trees protected from the sun's strongest rays. The cool mountain air and soil temperatures aid in their tolerance for withstanding high light levels. Recreating this scene in a lowland garden can be quite difficult and requires thoughtful site selection and proper soil preparation for success.

Alpine ferns require bright light levels with no hot sun, an open well-drained soil along with a steady supply of moisture, and a cool root run. Alpines can be worked into existing rock gardens by using rocks and shrubs to protect the delicate fronds from hot afternoon sun. The shady side of a house is an ideal location for a fern-friendly rock garden if it does not have additional tree cover. The open shady side of a house will provide bright open shade all day with little to no direct sunlight. Morning sun positions should provide shade by noon.

Soil preparation is as important as the exposure. Alpine ferns grow in rock soils with very good drainage that allows air to reach the roots. Adding coarse organic matter in gravelly soils helps hold moisture and nutrients. Snow-melt often provides wild ferns with a steady supply of moisture throughout most of the growing season. Replicating this may seem daunting, but is not difficult. Once the location is selected, build up the area with stones and a good alpine soil mix. Recipes for alpine soil mixes can be found online and local enthusiasts can help in selecting the right mix. A little trial and error will help refine the process. Keep organic matter to a minimum—no more than 10 to 20 percent of the soil mix. As compost breaks down, it turns into fine particles that clog air space. Any organic matter incorporated should be coarse. Composted bark or compost with the fine particles sifted out give the best results. The remainder of the mix should include materials that support good drainage, such as very coarse sand, grit, pumice, and fine gravel. These coarse materials can make up 50 to 90 percent of the soil mix, depending on your conditions.

Fortunately, there are some easy alpine species to try. One of the most satisfying is the evergreen *Asplenium trichomanes* (maidenhair spleenwort), native to mountains throughout the Northern Hemisphere. It can tolerate a wide variety of situations. If conditions are right, this species will populate the crevices with its offspring. Similar in appearance and in ease of cultivation is *Woodsia polystichoides* (holly fern woodsia), a choice deciduous fern. The bright green fronds are among the first to emerge in late winter to early spring, heralding the change of seasons.

Spreading ferns are often too rampant and soon outgrow rock gardens. Their long runners and brittle rhizomes can be quite difficult to remove completely without dismantling the entire garden. One of the few creeping ferns that should be considered is *Blechnum penna-marina* (little hard fern). This slow and low spreader is easy to control, and its bronzy new growth is brightest with some sun. As your confidence grows, species that are more difficult can be attempted and with a little luck enjoyed for years to come.

In regions with hot and humid summers and warm night temperature, it is difficult, if not impossible, to grow alpine species. This doesn't mean there are not interesting and choice plants for the rock garden. Gardeners in hotter areas should look to xeric or dryland species, many of which thrive in warmer conditions and have compact growth habits similar to those of the alpines. As an added feature, many xerics have exceptional foliage, with hairy scales (multicellular growths usually one cell thick) giving a fuzzy appearance to the frond or waxy leathery leaves with a beautiful blue or gray cast. The

Asplenium trichomanes 'Ramocristatum' and *Blechnum penna-marina* find ample nutrients and moisture between bricks.

Rockeries are perfect for showing off choice dwarf ferns.

American Southwest and northern Mexico have the highest diversity of xeric species, but dryland ferns can be found throughout the world.

Like most alpines, xeric ferns grow best with an even water supply during the growing season. Although they can tolerate considerable periods of drought, regular watering and fertilizer application makes for a fuller and more vigorous plant. These ferns need excellent drainage, much like alpines, and soil mixes used for alpine ferns generally suffice. Excessive winter wetness can kill xeric ferns. Mulching with about 1 inch (2.5 cm) of gravel or tucking the fern against a large rock with the roots under the rock helps keep the roots cool and the moisture even during the growing season and provides protection from excessive wetness while the fern is dormant. Try planting under roof eaves where regular rain does not reach. Some species, particularly those from the Southwest and Mexico, have a summer dormancy. These xerics should be allowed to dry out and not receive regular watering during this dormant period.

Start with a few easier-to-grow species. *Cheilanthes*, a genus synonymous with xeric ferns, offers two very easy choices for mild-winter regions, *C. tomentosa* (woolly lip fern), with soft fuzzy grayish green fronds, and the tiny *C. distans* (bristly lip fern), with short dark green narrow

fronds that stand straight up. Both of these dryland ferns slowly form small patches. The thin silvery fronds of *Astrolepis sinuata* (wavy cloak fern) make a compact and beautiful clump with an elegant upright habit, and this is a relatively easy xeric to please.

Gardeners from regions with colder winters can try *Cheilanthes lanosa* (hairy lip fern), a choice and hardy slow spreader with fuzzy scales that are a bit more green than gray. Those up to a challenge should try *Pellaea atropurpurea* (purple cliffbrake), a very hardy species with steely blue-green leaflets and dark purple wiry stems.

Many of these unusual specialty ferns are not widely available. Although it is tempting to collect a small division of a fern in the wild, this practice cannot be condoned. Most alpine and xeric ferns grow extremely slow in the wild and often live in a tenuous balance with the environment. Disruption, no matter how small, can cause a species to decline in the wild and rarely do wild plants survive in the garden.

HARDY FERNERIES

An interesting variation of the rockery is the fernery, a rockery entirely dedicated to ferns. Some of the first ferneries were built in tropical houses to display tender, newly introduced species from India, New Zealand, and Central and South America during the Victorian Era. Outdoors, however, ferneries may consist of attractively arranged stones and boulders, sometimes dramatically stacked, to create various microhabitats for the widest array of fern species and cultivars possible. Water features were often added to raise humidity and provide a home for water-loving ferns.

Cheilanthes bonariensis, a xeric fern with striking bluish pinnate fronds, growing at the University of California Botanical Garden at Berkeley.

Ferns for Rock Gardens

Adiantum aleuticum 'Subpumilum'
Asplenium platyneuron
Asplenium trichomanes and varieties
Astrolepis sinuata
Blechnum penna-marina
Cheilanthes species

Dryopteris affinis 'Crispa Gracilis'
Pellaea atropurpurea
Polypodium scouleri
Woodsia obtusa
Woodsia polystichoides

A pulhamite fern grotto
at Dewstow Gardens in
Caldicot, Wales.

During the Victorian era, where stone was scarce, industrious gardeners made their own stone with concretelike products. One of the most famous faux stone makers was James Pulham and Son, creators of pulhamite. Pulhamite garden features still dot the British landscape, with one of the most famous being Dewstow Gardens in South Wales. Its maze of tunnels, grottoes, and skillfully created false rock outcroppings create the perfect home for ferns. It is an excellent example of what creativity and imagination can add to a garden feature.

Hardy ferneries are best in a sheltered location with protection from winds and hot afternoon sun. Although the traditional material is rock, modern ferneries can be made of stackable pavers, terracotta, chimney liners, or hypertufa. Try to create some elevation change to have a more dramatic and interesting design. Humus-rich soil can be used to fill around the stones and provide a good medium for the ferns. Planting a fernery is an opportunity to combine various textures and forms in creative ways.

A spectacular fern grotto at Brodsworth Hall in West Yorkshire, England.

Epiphytic Ferns

In contrast to terrestrial ferns, which grow in the ground, epiphytic ferns grow on other plants or the remnants of plants, but are not parasitic and do not feed off the host plant. Although the term *epiphytic* is often applied to plants growing on rock, these are more correctly referred to as lithophytes. The genus *Polypodium* is mostly epiphytic or lithophytic in nature and can be found growing on trees, cliffs, and old stone walls and buildings.

Epiphytic ferns may look like they are growing without soil, but they are usually growing through a layer of moss covering a thin layer of decaying organic matter. The moss and organic matter help hold moisture and provide nutrients. Although epiphytic ferns are not easy to establish in the garden, a few techniques can help accomplish this. Most epiphytes and lithophytes can adapt to life on the ground if planted in well-drained soil.

The best time to establish epiphytic ferns in the garden is while they are dormant, just before they start to grow. The easiest way to start is to attempt to grow them on old logs or rotting stumps. Creeping ferns can be planted at the base and allowed to grow naturally on the wood over time. If the wood is rotted enough, a planting hole can be dug out of the soft wood and the fern planted in the hole. If a hole is dug in the wood, make sure it will drain to keep the newly planted fern from becoming waterlogged.

To establish epiphytic ferns on living trees, look for large branches or trunks that already have moss growing on the surface. Moss is a good indicator that the fern will grow well at the site. Branches and trunks devoid of moss are often too dry or too exposed to support ferns. Add a layer of moss followed by the unpotted and partially bare-rooted

Polypodium glycyrrhiza (licorice fern) thrives at the Elisabeth C. Miller Botanical Garden in Seattle, Washington.

fern. Carefully cover the fern roots with another layer of moss and then temporarily tie the moss and fern securely to the branch or trunk. Cotton twine or thin clear nylon string can be used. Check periodically to make sure the twine is not damaging the bark of the tree. It will take a few years for the fern to become fully attached on its own.

Growing ferns on walls and stone takes more perseverance from the gardener. For existing walls, little can be done to establish ferns on the sides other than to wait and hope. If the wall has a flat top, you can follow the same steps there as when establishing ferns on a tree. Once the top layer of moss is in place, secure it in place with stones set on top or by laying chicken wire over the top (when the fern is dormant) and securing the wire with masonry screws. For establishing ferns on stones, look for crevices where a pocket of soil can be added. Then plant in the crevice, packing around it with moss and compost. Smaller stones can be placed on top to hold the moss, soil, and compost while the fern establishes roots.

All epiphytic and lithophytic ferns appreciate additional watering the first few years. A slow-release fertilizer or an all-purpose organic fertilizer aids in their establishment.

Osmundastrum cinnamomeum (cinnamon fern) emerging along a pond in the Bellevue Botanical Garden in western Washington.

Osmunda regalis (royal fern), here at the Dallas Arboretum, can tolerate roots in standing water.

Ferns for Wet and Boggy Areas

Athyrium filix-femina
Dryopteris celsa
Dryopteris clintoniana
Dryopteris cristata
Dryopteris ludoviciana
Matteuccia
  struthiopteris
Onoclea sensibilis

Osmunda regalis
Osmundastrum
  cinnamomeum
Thelypteris palustris
Thelypteris simulata
Woodwardia areolata
Woodwardia virginica

Bog and Wetland Ferns

Moist conditions and ferns seem to go hand in hand, but surprisingly few ferns can tolerate their roots in standing water. Those that do thrive in boggy situations, along the water's edge, or where there is only an occasional high water table. Fortunately, these water lovers are easy to establish with little maintenance needed once growing.

Water-loving ferns can be divided into clumpers and spreaders. Clumping types are preferred for smaller garden ponds. Osmundas and their closely related kin, including *Osmunda regalis* (royal fern) and *Osmundastrum cinnamomeum* (cinnamon fern), create large dramatic long-lived clumps. These two ferns can tolerate roots in standing water. If the water table is a little lower, cultivars of *Athyrium filix-femina* (lady fern) and *Dryopteris filix-mas* (male fern), both deciduous species, can provide interesting forms and texture. Evergreen selections include *Cyrtomium falcatum* (holly fern) with bold shiny foliage, the resilient and colorful *D. erythrosora* (autumn fern), and the wide-spreading *D. expansa* (northern wood fern). Gardeners in regions with high heat and summer humidity should try *D. ludoviciana* (southern wood fern), which is known for its attractive deep green gleaming fronds, or perhaps *D. celsa* (log fern), a lush and upright grower. *Dryopteris ×australis* (Dixie wood fern), a hybrid of the aforementioned species, combines the best of both of its parents.

Spreading ferns are excellent choices for larger areas and for areas that occasionally flood. These plants can be vigorous growers, with dense fibrous root systems that hold soil in place and with running rhizomes that can quickly recolonize a washed out area. The most striking of the wetland spreaders is *Matteuccia struthiopteris* (ostrich fern), with tall perfectly formed shuttlecock growth that can form a sizable colony over time. Two attractive smaller spreaders are *Onoclea sensibilis* (sensitive fern), with interesting fertile fronds that last into winter, and *Thelypteris palustris* (marsh fern), with a fine delicate appearance and bright green foliage. A slightly less aggressive spreader is *Woodwardia areolata* (netted chain fern), with upright fronds that often have a red blush to the new spring growth. These colonizing ferns can be mixed with trees, shrubs, and perennials to create a network of soil-holding roots, with the spreading ferns weaving and tying together the planting.

Tree Ferns

Few ferns are more exciting to grow than tree ferns. Unfortunately, few tree ferns can be grown successfully outside of a frost-free climate. Gardeners in Zone 8, especially in mild coastal areas where frost is infrequent or light, can choose from most of the species listed in this book. With a fair amount of effort and luck, gardeners in colder regions can enjoy these treasured ferns until they grow too large to protect adequately.

The best species to start with is *Dicksonia antarctica* (Tasmanian tree fern), the hardiest tree fern that is readily available. It can be purchased as a young container-grown plant or as a cut log. Tree fern logs allow for a larger, more mature plant from the start and are easy to handle if growth on the log is dormant. Once growth starts on the log, care must be given to prevent breakage of the fronds. Logs should be soaked prior to planting. Soaked logs are quite heavy, so it may be wise to do this near the planting location.

Tree ferns do best in a sheltered location protected from strong winds with moderate to open shade. Tasmanian tree ferns tolerate morning sun, but can burn and dry out in hot afternoon sun. The soil should be rich and moisture retentive, with plenty of organic matter. Container-grown plants should be planted at the same depth as they were in the pot. The base of logs should be planted deep enough in the soil for the trunk to remain stable until new roots are established. Once the fern is planted, water it daily to keep it from drying out and to encourage root and frond growth.

Regular and thorough watering is critical to establishment of any tree fern. The trunk is composed of an outer layer of roots. It is important to not only water the soil surrounding the fern, but also to keep the trunk as moist as possible. Drip irrigation placed around the trunk just below the crown of fronds can help speed establishment and encourage the largest fronds. If the trunk does dry out, it is difficult to rehydrate. New plantings and small plants can be dug up and soaked in a tub of water. Larger ferns should have the trunks sprayed down several times a day for a few days until saturated.

Fertilizing is not necessary the first year in the ground and should only be done in late spring to mid-summer on established plants. Fertilizing late in the season can keep the fern from becoming fully dormant and encourages winter damage.

If winter temperatures drop below 28°F (−2°C), some winter protection is warranted. It is important to keep the crown relatively dry, while allowing moisture to reach the trunk. Small plants can be protected with a ring of burlap or landscape fabric staked around the trunk that reaches a little higher than the crown, then filled with straw or leaves. These should cover the top of the crown as well. Check periodically to make sure the trunk is still moist. If water needs to be added, avoid watering into the crown of the fern.

To protect larger ferns, many methods involve wrapping the trunk in various insulating materials with varying degrees of complexity. The key to all of these is to prevent freezing of the sensitive buds deep in the top crown. If your area has long protracted cold periods, the best method is to cut off the fronds, dig up the trunk, and overwinter the plant in a cold but relatively frost free garage or shed. Check occasionally to make sure the trunk does not dry out. The fronds will be smaller, but that is a small price to pay if the fern survives.

Drip irrigation keeps *Dicksonia antarctica* (Tasmanian tree fern) looking its best.

Fern Tables

A fun and creative way to enjoy ferns is to build a fern table, a sturdy structure with a flat surface that is covered with an assortment of ferns, small woodland plants, and moss. These plants are placed between and around interesting rocks and shapely pieces of wood. The result is a lovely woodland vignette that will fit into almost any garden.

Be creative when thinking about a fern table. It could be as simple as a very sturdy metal outdoor table with a concrete paver placed on top or as elaborate as a huge stone slab perched on boulders. The important point is that you need enough flat surface to add soil, plants, and stone and not have it dry out too quickly in summer. A 2 foot × 2 foot (60 cm × 60 cm) flat surface is the minimum required. Although larger is always better, the width should be no more than 4 feet (1.2 m), which will allow you to reach the center of the table easily for watering, weeding, and replacing plants in the future. It is best to build the table in place, as it can become quite heavy very quickly. A 2 foot × 2 foot (60 cm × 60 cm) hydro-pressed concrete paver makes a sturdy choice for a small table that is resistant to chipping and cracking and light enough that it can still be moved with a little muscle and a strong back.

Try to make the table look like a slice of the forest has been lifted and placed there for your viewing pleasure. Stones and interesting bits of wood add a natural woodland feel. This is a chance for your creativity to take over. Here are a few suggestions that will help tie it together.

Fern tables bring a woodland look to any garden.

- Incorporate local stone and wood. Robbing bits of these materials from other areas in the garden ties the table to the garden and the surrounding space.
- Use all the same type of stone or wood to lend continuity to the table. If each piece of stone or wood has a different color and texture, it is more difficult to make the table look cohesive.
- Look for weathered wood. Even rotting and overly weathered wood can add tremendously to the appearance of age.
- Select pieces with character. Although you don't want every piece to be filled with character, one or two pieces will lend interest. A section of heavily knotted rotting log mixed with a more mundane section of rotted log makes the eye focus on interesting forms presented. A prominently placed unusually shaped stone mixed with others of the same color and texture will achieve similar results.
- Place the rocks or wood in groups of odd numbers, starting with the largest and most interesting pieces and working down to the smallest piece.

SOIL MIX

The soil should be moisture retentive, but coarse enough for air to reach the roots. A good basic mix follows:

2 parts coarse compost
1 part medium to fine bark
1 part coarse sand
1 to 2 parts pea gravel

This soil mix is more natural looking than commercial mixes with pumice or perlite. Avoid perlite at all costs. Nothing destroys a nature planting more than bright white bits of perlite floating around on the surface. If you must use a commercial mix, use one that contains pumice. It is less noticeable in the finished table.

PLANTS

Medium to small ferns, those maturing less than 12 inches (30 cm) tall, are a great scale for fern tables. One or two larger ferns can be added for a focal point or as specimens. Even though ferns are the focus, you can accentuate the planting with dwarf shrubs, low and compact perennials, mini hostas, shade-tolerant dwarf conifers, and shade-loving saxifrages.

PUTTING IT ALL TOGETHER

Once the table is in place in a relatively flat level area, it can be planted. Start by lining the edges of the table with stones, pieces of wood, and clumps of moss to keep soil from washing off the sides when watering. Spread a light layer of soil over the base and then add the largest and most dramatic pieces of stone and wood on the table surface. Keep in mind that the soil in the center of the table when finished should be between 8 and 12 inches (20–30 cm) deep. Add more soil and then the two or three focal point plants.

Creating medleys of ferns and other plants makes the garden more interesting, and ferns especially add long-term interest.

At this point, you should have the general framework of the planting. Raise the height in the center by alternating between stones, pieces of wood, and plants until everything is in place. Add soil to fill pockets as necessary. To finish off the table, tuck moss between the plants, wood, and rock. Use moss collected from your own garden, because it is much more likely to thrive in the planting. Mosses collected from the wild often do not survive, and taking them can deplete native populations. Cover most of the soil surface with either moss or gravel. This helps hold the soil in place until the plant's roots can bind it all together. Once the planting is finished, give a gentle slow watering while making sure that the plants and soil have settled.

This masterful blend of perennials in John Massey's garden at Ashwood Nursery, West Midlands, England, includes *Athyrium niponicum* 'Pictum'.

Companion Plants for Ferns

The captivating foliage and diversity of textures offered by ferns open a door to endless arrays of pleasing garden vignettes and delightful combinations. Thoughtful combinations with ferns and other plants add aesthetic appeal and rhythm to the garden. The beauty of ferns will last for at least the growing season, and evergreen species can shine all year long, so it is important to have companion plants with a long season of interest. Look for plants with great foliage, excellent form, showy fruit, or autumn coloring. One of the first rules of combining plants with ferns is that foliage and form override flowers. There should be more to a perennial or shrub than just a nice bloom.

Although many plants mix well with ferns, a few seem to have been born to blend with ferns. Many of these originate from the same shady conditions and woodland environment that ferns grow in naturally. Others just have that certain something that truly resonates in the company of a fern. The five perfect companions for ferns are hostas, epimediums, hellebores, trilliums, and primroses. These readily available perennials give color, contrast, and offer interest almost year round. Beyond them is a long list of additional perennials, bulbs, and shrubs that work well with ferns. The best way to sort out this sea of plant possibilities is to consider the five complementary plant forms: bold-leaved companions, round or heart-shaped companions, plants with tall and willowy habits, plants with repeating patterns, and ephemerals. Choosing plants with one of these complementing shapes makes creating an attractive plant combo easy.

HOSTAS

Certainly, hostas are some of the most dramatic companion plants for ferns. The bold foliage plays well off the delicate and lacey fronds. Hostas have a wide range of colorful leaves that perfectly complements the green tones in ferns, and they can thrive on relatively little care. Large hostas are best with large robust ferns, creating big and dramatic plantings. Care must be given to mixing hostas with smaller ferns, however, as large hostas can eventually cover over and smother shorter ferns. The exception to this is ground-cover ferns. These can ramble below the hostas, adding a fine lace petticoat below the wide bold hosta leaves.

Medium and small hostas are excellent fern companions for container gardens. They are also best for grouping and mass planting. Try mini hostas with dwarf ferns in troughs, small containers, or fern tables.

Use selections with colorful foliage to your advantage. Blue-leaved hostas add the cooling tones ferns evoke. Dark green fern fronds make variegated hosta selections sparkle in the shade. Bright and bold white-and-green variegated hostas can be highlighted with the smoky purple and silver tones of *Athyrium niponicum* 'Pictum' (Japanese painted fern).

EPIMEDIUMS

This useful genus of perennial species has skyrocketed in popularity with the recent introduction of several new species and dozens of new cultivars. Epimediums are hardy and easy to grow and are becoming widely available. Most start flowering in early to mid-spring, with several spidery flowers dangling from thin but strong stems. The flower size can vary from less than 0.2 inch to nearly 2 inches (0.3–5 cm) across, but most are between 0.75 and 1 inch (1.8–2.5 cm) across. The foliage can be quite attractive, with each leaf composed of several leaflets, and the new growth can be as spectacular as the flowers. Leaf colors range from chocolate purple to burgundy, with red blushed or speckled and splashed patterns over bright green. A few choice epimediums also have deep burgundy to bright red edging the leaflets, highlighting their heart shape.

Give epimediums bright light to dappled shade for the best in flowers and foliage. Most clumping and slow-spreading selections are suitable with ferns. They can tolerate a wide range of soils as long as the drainage is adequate. Most epimediums prefer some extra water during prolonged dry periods, although a few exceptions are noted below.

Purists may prefer the species. Fortunately, many exceptional species make great fern companions. *Epimedium acuminatum* and *E. ×omeiense* are reliable low-growing evergreen species with large flowers mostly in shades of purple and white, but other color forms exist. The new growth can be pleasantly mottled in burgundy, and the foliage is evergreen. *Epimedium sempervirens* stays compact with medium to large flowers ranging from white to lavender or reddish purple. The foliage is evergreen, with a pleasing arrow-shaped leaflet. *Epimedium davidii* and *E. stellulatum* hold their flowers well above the foliage, making them particularly showy. *Epimedium davidii* has a long flowering period with bright canary yellow blooms, whereas *E. stellulatum* bears a profusion of bright white star-shaped flowers.

Epimedium grandiflorum and *E. ×youngianum* are particularly floriferous species. Both form tight clumps with numerous flowers in spring, then becoming a dense leafy mound. Both have many good cultivars, with flowers ranging from dark purple and rich reddish purple to lavender and white. The pale flowers stand out in the garden, but the dark rich purple tones are hard to resist. One of the most floriferous and vigorous of these selections is *E. grandiflorum* 'Lavender Lady'. The stems are loaded with large lavender-purple flowers followed by bright green leaves heavily blushed in wine red with green veins.

Epimedium ×youngianum 'Purple Heart' has slightly paler and smaller flowers that contrast nicely with the soft chocolate purple emerging foliage. A lovely compact Japanese selection with a fluffy more rounded bloom is the pinkish lavender *E. ×youngianum* 'Tamabotan'. Classic white-flowered *E. ×youngianum* 'Niveum' is an older selection with lightly bronzed new growth. More recent and more floriferous selections such as *E. ×youngianum* 'Milky Way' or *E. ×youngianum* 'White Star' are great substitutes, producing many more flowers than 'Niveum'. An interesting dwarf is *E. grandiflorum* 'Nanum'. The flowers rarely reach more than 4 inches (10 cm) high, and the new foliage is bright apple green boldly edged in rich red.

The deepest purple flower can be found on *Epimedium grandiflorum* 'Purple Prince'. Nearly black buds open to a dark grape purple with a touch of lavender-white on the tips of the spurlike petals. These contrast well with the lightly bronze-blushed new foliage. Sparkling reddish purple flowers can be found on *E. grandiflorum* 'Queen Esta',

One of the first rules of combining plants with ferns is that foliage and form override flowers.

Polystichum ×dycei combines beautifully with the dark purple–bronze foliage of *Epimedium grandiflorum* 'Queen Esta'.

E. grandiflorum 'Yubae' (also sold as 'Rose Queen'), and *E. ×youngianum* 'Ruby Tuesday'. The flowers of *E. grandiflorum* 'Queen Esta' glow among a profusion of dark purple-bronze foliage. The deeply colored flowers and foliage look great with the bright green fronds of *Athyrium filix-femina* (lady fern) cultivars or minty green fronds of the lady fern hybrid *Athyrium* 'Ghost'. *Epimedium grandiflorum* 'Yubae' and *E. ×youngianum* 'Ruby Tuesday' have a light bronzy blush to the new leaves, which combine well with ferns with golden or dark brown hairy-scaled stems. *Polystichum neolobatum* (Asian saber fern) or *Dryopteris cycadina* (shaggy shield fern) are perfect examples. Larger ferns with hairy scales, such as *D. wallichiana* (Wallich's wood fern), are better paired with a taller epimedium. A choice selection would be *E. grandiflorum* 'Red Queen', which reaches up to 2 feet (60 cm) in height with spectacular and large bright reddish purple blooms.

Hybridizing and selecting of superior seedlings has generated a wealth of new cultivars that blend prolonged and abundant blooms with excellent flowers. Orange-tinted yellow flowers float high above the red-speckled green leaves of *Epimedium* 'Amber Queen'. This fine plant has reoccurring flowers that last well into summer. If yellow is not your color, try *E.* 'Pink Champagne'. It has many of the fine qualities of 'Amber Queen', but the flowers are light pink with a rose-pink center. Very robust and garden-worthy is *E.* 'Lavender Cascade', an early bloomer that produces an abundance of lavender-purple flowers just above the shiny green heart-shaped leaflets strikingly edged in reddish purple.

A few drought-tolerant slow-spreading epimediums can be used with ferns that receive limited watering. The older well-tested *Epimedium ×rubrum* has small but charming red and white flowers with red-blushed new growth. Its recent selection 'Sweetheart' has very large leaflets edged with a thin line of red. *Epimedium ×warleyense* and *E.* 'Black Sea' have unique orange flowers with attractive evergreen leaves. With some sun, the winter foliage of 'Black Sea' turns an inky purple until spring. Use these tough selections with larger, hardy ferns that will not be crowded out as these epimediums spread. *Dryopteris filix-mas* (male fern) and *D. affinis* (golden-scaled male fern) both hold their own against encroachment.

The bold leaves of hellebores contrast well with *Polystichum setiferum* Plumosomultilobum Group (plumose soft shield fern).

HELLEBORES

Hellebores are not only useful for their winter and early-spring blooms, but many are lovely foliage plants as well. These easy-to-grow perennials tolerate a wide range of soil conditions and do not outcompete neighboring plants. The most widely available is *Helleborus ×hybridus* (Lenten rose). Considerable breeding work has been done to produce a broad range of flower colors and various flower forms, including fully double forms. The flowers emerge in mid to late winter or early spring, nodding in small clusters at the end of the stems to protect them from the harsh weather. Lenten roses are gloriously colorful at a time when little else is happening in the garden. As the flowers open, the foliage develops in a bold hand-shaped form, with deeply cut lobes providing a striking counterpoint to most ferns during the growing season.

Protected locations are suitable for *Helleborus niger* (Christmas rose), which is smaller than other hellebores and can be used with slow-growing and small to medium ferns. It starts blooming in early to mid-winter with large pure white flowers that are held facing outward. The Christmas rose is an excellent companion to evergreen ferns.

Three stemmed species are commonly available, *Helleborus argutifolius* (Corsican hellebore), *H. ×sternii* (Stern's hybrid hellebore), and *H. foetidus*. *Helleborus argutifolius* and *H. ×sternii* are closely related and have similar habits and appearances. Both flower in the winter with chartreuse to reddish pink–blushed green blooms on long stems. The flowers complement the lovely foliage, which can be a grayish to medium green with spiny edged leaflets. Both of these species are best with larger ferns. The stems can become floppy in shaded conditions, but once flopped over the plant can be woven through smaller ferns for a contrasting leaf texture. The unfortunately named *H. foetidus* (stinking hellebore) thrives in the woodland and has lovely deeply cut dark green leaves on sturdy stems. Vibrant green flowers form in clusters at the stem ends, opening in early to mid-winter. The stinking hellebore works well with mounding and widely arching ferns and does not crowd out small or less vigorous ferns.

TRILLIUMS

Where trilliums grow, ferns are sure not to be too far away. In the garden, the taller and more vigorous *Trillium* species are the best choices. These excellent garden plants emerge early and provide color just before new fern fronds start to grow. If the fern is cut back in late winter, trilliums can fill the spaces between. As the fronds expand and fully develop by early summer, many trilliums are going dormant for the season.

Trillium grandiflorum is hard to beat, with its large gleaming white flowers and easy cultivation. This eastern North American native is adaptable to many parts of the world. Gardeners in locations with mild winters and cool summers can try the western North American counterpart, *T. ovatum*. In both of these species, the flower fades to pink as it ages. Other exceptional plants to try are *T. erectum*, *T. vaseyi*, and *T. flexipes*.

Sessile trilliums have flowers with no stem to attach them directly to the leaf. Generally, these unusual flowers point upward like a candle flame and are often complemented with interesting mottled leaves. A few of them are widely available, including *Trillium sessile* and *T. cuneatum*, with variable dark red, yellowy-green to brown upright blooms, and the yellow-flowered and lemon-scented *T. luteum*, all eastern North American natives. Some of the largest and most spectacular sessile trilliums are the western U.S. species *T. chloropetalum*, *T. albidum*, and the choice *T. kurabayashii*.

Trilliums are plants of patience; it can take between five to seven years for a seed to sprout and grow into a flowering plant. Their slow growth makes it tempting to collect these treasures from the wild, but this should be firmly discouraged. Native colonies can be quickly depleted and are very slow to recover, and many species are rare and may be protected under state or federal laws. Nursery-grown plants represent the best choice for the garden.

PRIMROSES

Primroses herald spring. They can be a foil surrounding evergreen ferns or add a splash of color prior to the new fronds emerging. Late-spring and early-summer bloomers add a dainty presence to the fresh new fern growth. Many choice garden selections have a wide range of colors and an extended bloom time coupled with an ease of cultivation. Most primroses prefer bright open shade or partial sun, good soil conditions, and regular watering during dry periods. Nearly all primroses share the fern's resentment of hot midday and afternoon sun.

Polystichum neolobatum (Asian saber fern) and *Trillium ovatum* in the Steffen/Peterson garden.

Candelabra primrose growing among ferns at the Bellevue Botanical Garden in northern Washington.

The well-known European natives *Primula vulgaris*, *P. veris*, and *P. elatior* all have charming early flowers, mostly in shades of yellow, but other color forms can be found. Polyanthus primroses, a hybrid group, offer a huge range of bright colors on compact plants. The inexpensive splashy primroses most commonly available in late winter and spring are good for a season of color, but are usually poor quality as a perennial. With a little searching, gardeners can find superior perennial forms of polyanthus primrose that will thrive for years in the garden.

Another hybrid group for early spring is the Wanda hybrids. Derived from *Primula juliae*, these easy-to-grow compact and vigorous plants generally bloom in shades of magenta, pink, or lavender-purple. Use these early bloomers to give color before the fronds emerge on deciduous ferns.

Primula sieboldii, an exceptional early bloomer from Japan, has relatively small flowers in clusters atop 6- to 10-inch (15- to 25-cm) stems in soft pastel pink, purple, and white. This primrose is very useful for filling the bare areas left once evergreen ferns have been cut back in late winter. It starts growing soon after ferns have been cut back, flowers prior to the new fronds emerging, and then goes dormant in early summer as the new fronds fully expand.

Wet and moist areas are perfect for many of the later-blooming candelabra primroses. These are generally easy to grow and once established they often reseed, creating breathtaking drifts of color. Candelabra primroses are tall growers and offer a vertical element against arching fronds.

PLANTS WITH BOLD LEAVES

Large leaves with bold shapes are dramatic and add a strong contrast when mixed with ferns. They draw the eye and keep your attention, making a great specimen or a focal point in the garden. When using plants with bold foliage, try to keep a sense of scale, as leaves too large can overwhelm neighboring plants.

Rodgersia is a genus of deciduous perennials with large hand-shaped or feathery leaves. Several cultivars have attractive bronzy new growth. Most rodgersias reach about 3 feet (0.9 m) tall in leaf and can spread to 5 or 6 feet (1.5–1.8 m) wide over time. In early summer, tall plumelike flowering stems reach 4 to 6 feet (1.2–1.8 m) and are topped with hundreds of tiny white to pink blooms. Do not rush to deadhead after flowering, as the maturing seed heads of many cultivars turn an attractive bright maroon red.

A perennial with a similar stature is *Diphylleia cymosa* (umbrella leaf), a choice ornamental from the southeastern United States that bears attractive blue fruits on brilliant red stems. It is slow to emerge in spring, but the stems reach 3 or 4 feet (0.9–1.2 m) tall, opening with one or two large rounded leaves edged with broad pointed lobes. Flowering stems have an umbrella-like cluster of white flowers that mature in late summer to powder blue berries. As the berries mature, the flowering stems turn scarlet red.

A truly magnificent perennial for a bold statement is *Aralia cordata* (Japanese spikenard). This tall grower can reach 6 to 8 feet (1.8–2.4 m), with thick strong stems supporting large compound leaves that can reach close to 3 feet (0.9 m) in length. In midsummer, clusters of small white flowers are held above the foliage, later turning to showy black berries. Bright golden foliage forms exist and stay slightly smaller when mature.

Arisaema adds a little surprise in the garden. Commonly called jack-in-the-pulpit or cobra lily, these unusual bulbs are woodland natives and thrive in shade. There are many different species to choose from, ranging in height from 12 inches (30 cm) to 5 or 6 feet (1.5–1.8 m). Their unusual hooded blooms are intriguing, if not beautiful, mostly in shades of green, white, brown, and dark burgundy. The foliage is large and, depending on the species, can look like an oversized trillium leaf or a finely divided umbrella. Arisaemas do poorly in wet soil while they are dormant, but require regular watering during growth. Try planting under the foliage of evergreen ferns to keep the bulbs dry during the winter dormancy. Have patience. These bulbs can be slow to emerge in the spring, waiting until the soil temperatures warm.

PLANTS WITH ROUND AND HEART-SHAPED LEAVES

Rounded and heart-shaped leaves are the complete opposite of lacey fern fronds, which makes them contrasting companions (apparently, opposites do attract). Many shade-garden perennials have these foliage shapes, with two very common plants being *Brunnera macrophylla* (Siberian bugloss) and *Asarum* (wild ginger). Siberian bugloss has several cultivars selected for variegation on the wide heart-shaped leaf. Most are variations of silver mottling, with one of the most notable being *B. macrophylla* 'Jack Frost'. This deciduous perennial starts growing early in the year, with thin delicate flower stems sporting sprays of blue or white flowers reminiscent of old-fashioned forget-me-nots. The flowers are soon followed by the lush foliage.

Wild ginger is an aristocrat of the shade garden. The lovely refined foliage is typically a deep rich green and can be tastefully etched in silver. Several species and cultivars are available, many of them evergreen, and nearly all have distinctive fragrant spicy foliage that is particularly noticeable when brushed against. Wild gingers stay under 6 to 8 inches (15–20 cm) tall and grow best in shade with humus-rich, well-drained soil. Clumping and spreading selections can be found. Clumping forms are best around small and slow-growing ferns.

Few think of begonias as being hardy, but the resilient *Begonia grandis* is tolerant of both heavy freezing and hot humid summers. Typically not flowering until mid or late summer, it can reach 2 to 3 feet (60–90 cm) and is topped with white or pink flowers

Bold leaves and tree ferns create a
compelling view in the Treganowan
garden, London.

until the first hard frost. The foliage is dark green on the top surface with an underside of green veined in red or solid maroon. With proper backlighting, the foliage glows blood red in the evening sun. Over time *B. grandis* can form a sizable colony, but it is easy to limit to a small area.

Three lesser-known but equally ornamental companions are *Beesia deltophylla*, *Saruma henryi*, and *Pachyphragma macrophylla*. *Beesia deltophylla* is a relatively new shade-loving perennial that is proving to be an exceptional addition to the landscape. There is some doubt as to the identity of this plant, which is also sold under the name *B. calthifolia*. Regardless of the name, the foliage is beautiful and reminiscent of a shiny violet leaf. The dark green leaf is broken by the attractive netting of pale yellowish green veins. The shiny reflective qualities of the leaves are luminescent in darker areas in the garden. The plant grows 12 to 15 inches (30–38 cm) tall, with a slightly greater spread. Thin willowy flower spikes appear in late spring and early summer, reaching about 2 feet (60 cm) tall with small white blooms.

Glossy *Beesia deltophylla* leaves are a wonderful complement for delicate *Adiantum venustum*.

Saruma henryi (upright wild ginger) has leaves similar to those of true wild ginger (*Asarum*), a distant relative. The leaf is pale green and velvety from short soft hairs covering the surface. Upright stems reach 18 to 24 inches (45–60 cm) tall with a spread that is slightly less. Small triangular primroselike yellow flowers dot the upper foliage through the summer.

The round ruffled leaves of *Pachyphragma macrophylla* form loose rosettes of evergreen foliage about 18 inches (45 cm) across and 15 inches (38 cm) tall. From late winter to midspring, a spray of bright snow-white blooms brightens the shade garden. This tough plant is drought tolerant and easy to grow. Established plants can seed about the garden, but excess seedlings are easily weeded out with little effort. A more restrained and compact groundcover for small areas is *Cardamine trifolia*, with trifoliate evergreen leaves and delicate tiny white flowers in early spring.

PLANTS WITH TALL AND WILLOWY HABITS

Upright foliage or stems and narrow willowy leaves offer a soft contrast to lax fern foliage. The vertical lines created by upright growers like *Polygonatum* (Solomon's seal) or the late-blooming *Tricyrtis* (toad lily) interrupt the horizontal and arching lines of ferns. Some perennials have upright stems partially cloaked with horizontal foliage. For example, *Actaea simplex* and *A. racemosa* can reach 5 to 6 feet (1.5–1.8 m) tall and bear fragrant flowers in late summer.

Plants with willowy foliage provide a very subtle contrast to ferns. Grasses and sedges provide this contrast along with a sense of movement, even with a light breeze. Select green- or blue-foliaged species for a natural look. Several variegated selections add color and brightness. Two bright golden choices are *Hakonechloa macra* 'Aureola' (golden Japanese forest grass) and *Carex oshimensis* 'Evergold' (variegated Japanese sedge).

Stems of *Polygonatum multiflorum* (Solomon's seal) arch through *Athyrium filix-femina* 'Minutissimum' (dwarf lady fern).

PLANTS WITH REPEATING PATTERNS

Companion plants can also play off the geometric patterns of fern fronds. The symmetry of ferns and the repeated patterns in the frond are beautiful when mixed with other plants with geometric patterns, and the effect is maximized with groupings. The evergreen dwarf saxifrage *Saxifraga* 'Primuloides' has tight succulent-like rosettes that would be a perfect groundcover under a small fern. Repetitive circular patterns of rosettes and leaves contrast with the angular frond lines, yet harmonize with the repeating patterns.

A similar feel can be achieved in larger spaces through the use of the spreading groundcovers like the evergreen spurge *Euphorbia amygdaloides* var. *robbiae*, *Oxalis oregano* (redwood sorrel), of which the evergreen selections are particularly garden worthy, or *Maianthemum stellatum* (star-flowered false Solomon's seal) with pointed leaflets.

EPHEMERALS

Once evergreen ferns have been cut back in winter, the open bare soil of the garden can look a little desolate. Spring ephemerals and early-season bulbs are a beautiful solution to fill this seasonal gap until the fresh fronds emerge. Ephemerals are perennials that grow quickly, bloom, and then return to dormancy in a short period. Many of these plants prefer some sun or open shade, making them particularly useful under deciduous trees.

Anemone nemorosa (wood anemone) and *A. blanda* (Grecian windflower) are classic ephemerals that slowly form low green carpets laden with white, pink, or purple daisylike flowers. Some ephemerals are as useful for their foliage as their early bloom, with *Sanguinaria canadensis* (bloodroot) and *Erythronium* (dogtooth violet) being striking examples. Early smaller bulbs, including the bright blue bells of *Scilla siberica* (Siberian squill), the luminescent lavender cups of *Crocus tommasinianus* (affectionately known as "tommies"), and the stark white nodding flowers of *Galanthus* (snowdrop), add their color and then disappear once the ferns start growing. Hardy cyclamen can provide not only adorable flowers in pink, magenta, and white, but also a fine array of silver-patterned leaves that light up dry and heavily shaded areas through the winter.

Seedheads of a species tulip poke through *Polypodium ×mantoniae* 'Cornubiense'.

Gymnocarpium disjunctum (western oak fern) and *Achlys triphylla* (vanilla leaf) provide contrasting geometric patterns.

UNDERSTANDING FERNS

It is easy to imagine what a fern is, but frustratingly vague to define this diverse group. Like trees and flowering plants, ferns have leaves, stems, and roots, but unlike them, ferns are flowerless and do not produce seeds. Instead, ferns produce spores (one-celled reproductive units). This distinction sets them apart from all flowering and cone-bearing plants. It is also a telltale sign of the ancient lineage of this plant group. Mosses, another ancient plant group, also bear spores but, unlike ferns, they lack the xylem and phloem vessels that move water and nutrients between the roots and leaves.

Much scientific work has been performed regarding the origin and evolution of ferns. The oldest fern fossil, housed at the Queensland Museum in Australia, dates back approximately 375 million years. Remarkably, this places ferns coming onto the scene only a scant 50 million years after the first land plants. Not surprisingly, these early species no longer exist today, but we can have a direct link to ancient history in our gardens.

The title for the oldest living fern species is disputed between two closely related ferns, *Osmundastrum* (formerly *Osmunda*) *cinnamomeum* (cinnamon fern) and *Osmunda claytoniana* (interrupted fern). Fossils found in western Canada were confirmed to be the cinnamon fern and date back to approximately 75 million years, which firmly establishes this fern as dinosaur food. As for *O. claytoniana*, it appears to be identical to *O. claytoniites*, which is known from fossils discovered in Antarctica dating back 200 million years.

Dryopteris filix-mas (male fern) sits at the edge of a pool in John Massey's garden at Ashwood Nursery, West Midlands, England.

If this ever proved true, it means that *O. claytonia* is older than *Osmundastrum cinnamomeum* and would have existed when the great continent Pangaea began to split into Gondwana and Laurasia, the very beginnings of our present-day world.

Great science often leads to great change, and this is true with ferns. The ability to use DNA for exploring plant relationships has led to several shifts in the way ferns are categorized with regard to each other and to all plants. One of the most profound and unfortunate changes is that the beloved plant group Pteridophyta, which included spikemosses, clubmosses, quillworts, horsetails, and all manner of ferns, is no longer considered a valid group. It is now replaced by the less nostalgic Monilophyta. Monilophytes include all plants that we think of as ferns, while also including horsetail as a fern. Spikemosses, clubmosses, and quillworts are left to the lesser evolved Lycophyta. Even though this change will slowly permeate the literature, it will be hard to think of fern lovers as monilologists or that we can suffer from monilomania.

A young plant of *Polystichum setiferum* Plumosomultilobum Group

Parts of a Fern

The construction of ferns is remarkably simple. Almost all ferns are made up of three parts: roots, stems, and leaves. The various combinations of these parts have developed into a multitude of forms. On most hardy ferns, we only see the leaves. The roots are where we expect them to be, below ground, but often so is the stem. The stems and leaves of ferns are typically referred to by specialized names, along with the various features attached to them. There is also an array of descriptive names for the variations of the leaves, all of which is necessary to describe the complexity of these marvelous plants.

ROOTS

It is always best to start from the ground up. Roots form the foundation of any plant. Fern roots tend to have a very consistent appearance, especially in hardy ferns: they are generally wiry and dark brown or black and may have a creamy to whitish tip, often with a fuzzy appearance from the abundance of root hairs. Roots anchor the plant and absorb water and nutrients through the fine root hairs.

STEMS

Stems are often an elusive feature of ferns and are typically presented in a modified and less recognizable form than what most gardeners are used to seeing. The woody twigs of trees and shrubs or the succulent stems of perennials are a much more familiar vision of plant support. Tree ferns seem to have a clear stem, commonly referred to as the trunk, but the real stem is mostly hidden under a layer of strong fibrous roots and the remains of old fronds.

Most hardy fern stems develop as rhizomes. This stem variation can easily be confused for roots, but rhizomes serve the same function as the stems of all plants, to support the leaves. Rhizomes are stems that usually grow horizontally and can be fully or partially underground. They can be hairy, scaly (covered with scales), or covered in fibrous roots. They can be thin and wiry or as thick as a tree trunk, but nearly all of these variations can fall into four major growth patterns: short-creeping, long-creeping, erect, or tufted.

Dryopteris affinis crosier

Rachis

Blade

Frond

Stipe

Ferns with short-creeping rhizomes generally form tight clumps, with excellent examples being *Dryopteris erythrosora* (autumn fern) and *Adiantum pedatum* (common maidenhair). Long-creeping rhizomes are features associated with groundcover ferns. Typical examples include *Gymnocarpium dryopteris* (oak fern) and the rampageous *Pteridium aquilinum* (bracken fern). Ferns with erect rhizomes become graceful arching vase-shaped clumps. Fronds arise from around a central thick stem and over time often develop a short stubby trunk; *Polystichum polyblepharum* (tassel fern) and *Dryopteris filix-mas* (male fern) are common ferns with this type of stem. Most ferns with erect rhizomes have an architecturally striking habit. Tufted rhizomes spread horizontally but occasionally send up erect branches, or tufts, resulting in a plant that forms colonies of lovely vase-shaped ferns. The most notable example is *Matteuccia struthiopteris* (ostrich fern).

LEAVES (CROSIERS, FIDDLEHEADS, FRONDS)

The leaf is the most interesting and diverse part of a fern, and consequently it is riddled with specialized terminology and often multiple Latinized descriptors. Some of these terms are more commonly used by botanists and serious fern collectors, whereas others are more common with the general gardener. Frond is one of the few terms used by both botanists and gardeners to refer to the entire leaf. From the tip of the leaf to where the leaf attaches to the stem (rhizome) is the frond. When the frond first emerges and starts to unfurl, botanists refer to it as a crosier, although many a gardener call this a fiddlehead.

The frond is divided into two parts, the blade and the stipe. The blade is the leafy part of the frond. The rachis stretches the entire length of the frond, but the lower part below the leaf is more properly called the stipe. The stipe is the part of the leaf stem that connects the leafy parts to the rhizome. The stipe can also quite correctly be referred to as a petiole or stalk.

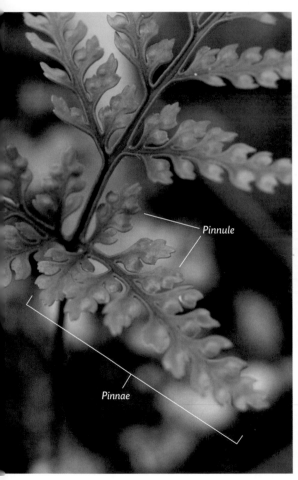

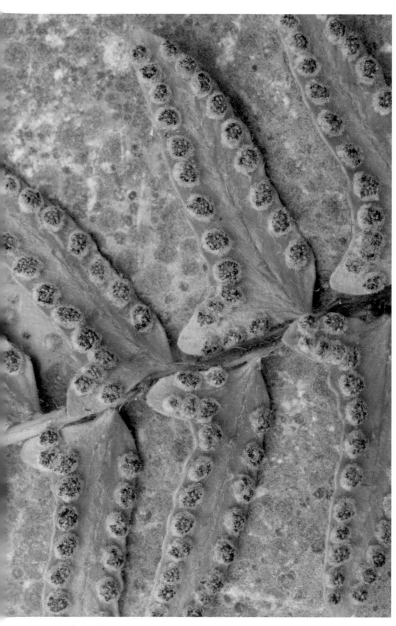

Sori of *Woodsia polystichoides*

The blade consists of two major parts, the rachis or stem and the leaf. The leaf can be in numerous shades and sizes. The blade can appear as one complete leaf, referred to as a simple leaf. An example of this is the tropical *Asplenium nidus* (bird's nest fern), a common houseplant. Most ferns have divided foliage that is commonly referred to as a compound leaf. Each leaf division off the rachis is called a pinna (pl. pinnae). The midrib or main stem running through a pinna is called a costa. If a pinna is further divided, each leaflet division off the costa is called a pinnule (pl. pinnules). The midrib of a pinnule is called a costule.

Much of the way that pinnae and pinnules are structurally divided can be described in five unique ways: simple (entire, undivided, with smooth margins), forked, palmate (like a hand), pinnatifid (deeply lobed but not cut to the axis), and pinnate (having pinnae in rows on both sides of an axis, once divided). Individual fronds can be composed of one or more of these divisions, leading to nearly endless and exciting diversity for fern enthusiasts. For example, bipinnate fronds are twice divided, tripinnate are three times divided, quadripinnate are four times divided, and so on. Pinnate-pinnatifid fronds are once divided with deeply lobed pinnae, but not cut to the midrib, bipinnate-pinnatifid fronds are twice divided with deeply lobed pinnae, but not cut to the midrib, and tripinnate-pinnatifid fronds are three times divided with deeply lobed pinnae, but not cut to the midrib.

Understanding the differences of these five variations provides a gateway to understanding the complex Latinized descriptions of many Victorian fern cultivars still available today. If this seems overwhelming, start with familiar ferns and carefully study the frond arrangements. These small beginning steps will build the knowledge, confidence, and taxonomic tools to tackle the more complex cultivars.

Sori (singular sorus) are groups of spore-bearing structures usually on the underside of the frond. Their color and arrangement can be significant in identifying the genus to which a fern belongs.

LEAF FORMS

ENTIRE: *Asplenium scolopendrium*

FORKED: *Polypodium vulgare* 'Bifidocristatum'

PALMATE: *Pyrrosia polydactyla*

PINNATIFID: *Asplenium pinnatifidum*

PINNATE: *Cyrtomium fortunei*

BIPINNATE-PINNATIFID: *Woodwardia unigemmata*

TRIPINNATE: *Onychium japonicum*

BIPINNATE: *Polystichum polyblepharum*

PLANT FORMS

ANGUSTATE(UM), NARROW: *Dryopteris affinis* 'Cristata Angustata'

CONGESTA(UM), CROWDED: *Polystichum setiferum* 'Congestum Cristatum'

CONTORTA, TWISTED: *Pyrrosia lingua* 'Eboshi'

CRISPA(UM), CURLED LIKE HAIR: *Dryopteris crispifolia*

CRISTATA(UM), CRESTED: *Pyrrosia lingua* 'Futaba Shishi'

CRUCIATE, CROSSED: *Athyrium filix-femina* 'Dre's Dagger'

FIMBRIATE, FRINGED: *Asplenium scolopendrium* Fimbriata Group

FOLIOSE, LEAFY: *Athyrium filix-femina* Foliose Group

PLANT FORMS (CONTINUED)

GRANDICEPS, WITH A LARGE HEAD: *Athyrium filix-femina* Grandiceps Group

INCISA(UM), SLASHED: *Asplenium trichomanes* 'Incisum'

LACERATE(UM), TORN: *Polypodium cambricum* 'Omnilacerum Oxford'

PLUMOSE, FEATHERY: *Polystichum setiferum* Plumosum Group

POLYDACTYLA, MANY-FINGERED: *Athyrium filix-femina*
Mediodeficiens Group

RAMOSE(UM), BRANCHED: *Coniogramme intermedia* 'Shishi'

UNDULATE(UM), WAVY: *Asplenium scolopendrium*
Undulate Group

Distinguishing Characteristics of the Genera

Here we provide a guide to pronunciation and one of the best features for identifying each fern genus. Other ferns may share some of these features, but these genera are the ones most often found in gardens and nurseries.

Adiantum (ad-ee-AN-tum): Pinnae fan or wedge shaped. Sori around the outer edges covered with a false indusium (a small membrane or tissue covering the sori) of curled segments.

Asplenium (as-PLEE-nee-um): Sori in herringbone pattern. Fronds evergreen.

Athyrium (ah-THEE-ree-um): Sori covered with half-moon-shaped indusium. Fronds deciduous.

Blechnum (BLEK-num): Some species dimorphic with fertile fronds erect. Sori linear, occupying entire space from midrib to outer edge of fertile frond segment. Indusium linear with central lengthwise opening (slit down the middle).

Asplenium trichomanes

Adiantum aleuticum 'Subpumilum'

Athyrium filix-femina

Blechnum wattsii

Cyrtomium falcatum

Cyrtomium (sir-TOE-mee-um): Foliage leathery, bold, evergreen. Sori with peltate (umbrella-shaped) indusium.

Dryopteris (dry-OP-ter-is): Sori with kidney-shaped indusium.

Osmunda (oz-MUN-duh): Dimorphic fronds. Spores held in clusters of round sporangia (spore-bearing structures). Ripe spores turn olive green; deciduous.

Polypodium (pol-ee-PO-dee-um): Often epiphytic. Leaves leathery, usually pinnate. Sori large and round. No indusium. Spore ripens a bright yellow or orange.

Polystichum (pol-IS-tik-um): Upward ear on the pinnae, commonly called a thumb. Sori covered with peltate (centrally attached) indusium.

Woodwardia (wood-WAR-dee-ah): Sori arranged in long lines like strings of sausage or a sown chain stitch (hence chain fern).

Osmunda regalis 'Purpurascens'

Polystichum munitum

Woodwardia unigemmata

Dryopteris affinis

Polypodium vulgare

140 FERNS
FOR THE
GARDEN

ADIANTUM
Maidenhair fern

The maidenhairs are popular and beautifully irresistible, delicate-appearing plants that evoke the traditional image of fern in the mind's eye of the gardening public. Some 150 to 200 species are scattered over the world's various fern habitats with many in the American tropics. The genus name comes from the Greek *adiantos*, to shed water, and refers to the water-repellant foliage.

These ferns are easily recognized by fronds with glossy, brittle dark stipes and tissue-thin wedge-shaped pinnae. Fan-shaped, horizontal blades are familiar hallmarks but triangular foliage is also common. Spores are produced marginally in sori protected under an in-rolled false indusium. Some species are apogamous, producing new plants without sexual fertilization.

The maidenhairs are prized for their decorative properties indoors or out. In the temperate garden, they offer sylvan charm in filtered shade and moist compost and despite their delicate appearance are dependable ornamentals. (Houseplant enthusiasts, however, often bemoan their performance.)

Plant your collections, indoors or out, in a potting mix of light composty soil and enough gritty additives to ensure good drainage. Containerized maidenhairs do not like to be overpotted, so choose a container just larger than the rootball. When it is time to transplant, move to the next larger sized pot with no more than 1 inch (2.5 cm) of fresh soil around the perimeter.

All said, your garden maidenhairs should provide years of decoration.

Adiantum aleuticum

Western maidenhair

TYPE AND SIZE Deciduous, 18–30 inches (45–75 cm) tall

HARDINESS Zones 3–8

DISTINCTIVE FEATURES Rhizome is short-creeping, producing foliar fans on upright, blackish stipes. Unlike the extremely closely related (and former namesake) *A. pedatum*, *A. aleuticum* produces green, not rosy, new growth. The stipes fork into two radiating and continuous branches. A close look may reveal a single fan-shaped pinnule on the rachis between the fork and the first pinnae. This is frequently present on *A. aleuticum* but rarely seen on *A. pedatum*. Outward-fanning pinnae form pedate (hand-shaped) blades with an extended middle finger swirling horizontally to 1 foot (30 cm).

ORIGIN AND HABITAT Western maidenhair prefers light shade in moist, rich woodland duff in coastal areas from Alaska to California. The species forms carpets in forests, thrives in humid ravines and by streamsides, occasionally colonizes shady road banks, and may settle on vertical cliffs.

GARDEN AND DESIGN USES This fern is easily grown in western U.S. gardens, presenting a welcome and calming atmosphere often associated with tranquil woodland experiences. The graceful airy fronds make it a natural choice for streamsides or as a soft complement to enhance water features everywhere. It takes time to establish in the eastern United States, where *A. pedatum* is a more appropriate option. New growth appears on *A. aleuticum* a week or two later than that on *A. pedatum* and, by balance, remains green for several weeks longer in autumn.

SELECTIONS

'Imbricatum' Overlapping pinnae give a sculptured, layered effect to this handsome understory variety, which ranges in height from 8 to 12 inches (20–30 cm); part shade. Zones 3–8.

'Subpumilum' ▶ A highly desirable dwarf maidenhair, 4–6 inches (10–15 cm), that was discovered in the 1960s by the late Seattle horticulturist and botanist Carl English, on sea cliffs on the west coast of Vancouver Island, British Columbia. He generously shared spores so that this little plant could be distributed to enthusiasts throughout the country. With varying designations in the nomenclature, it has been a bit of an orphan botanically, but it is truly a dwarf worth adopting. While suitable for Zones 6–8, it is unfortunately not the easiest to introduce. Contented plants are often in vertical plantings with good drainage in part sun to light shade (smaller in part sun). Others treat them as an ornamental foreground cover or in mixed container plantings. It does not tolerate heavy soil.

Adiantum japonicum Synonyms *A. aleuticum* var. *japonicum* and *A. pedatum* var. *japonicum*. Deciduous, 1 foot (30 cm), handsome bright rosy new growth, pedate (hand-shaped) fronds, shade, Japan. Interplant with either *A. aleuticum* or *A. pedatum* to create a charming and picturesque tapestry. Zones 6–9.

Adiantum capillus-veneris

Southern maidenhair, Venus-hair fern

TYPE AND SIZE Deciduous, 12–18 inches (30–45 cm) tall
HARDINESS Zones 7 (with protection) to 10
DISTINCTIVE FEATURES Rhizome is short-creeping, producing mounds of triangular bipinnate blades with dark-stalked, wedge-shaped, drooping pinnules. This species reproduces with ease (and at random) from spores and willingly from division.
ORIGIN AND HABITAT One of the world's most widely distributed maidenhairs, *A. capillus-veneris* is native to tropical and warm-temperate zones as well as sites where cold winters are balanced by hot summers. Plants like limestone and make delightful displays as pendulous curtains of lace in moist seeps, such as in Zion National Park, or as airy and beautiful groundcovers elsewhere. Many excellent named cultivars offer variety to the garden's palette.
GARDEN AND DESIGN USES This fern will do well in shady bright to dim light and is an excellent choice for adding buoyancy to woodland landscapes. Let it drift through taller shrubbery, where it will give plumy unity to the entire planting. It is also widely grown as a houseplant.
SELECTIONS
'Falling Waters' ▲ Slightly smaller than the type (10 inches, 25 cm) and cold tolerant to single digits in areas with hot summers.
'Fan Dance' Tightly bunched foliage to 6 inches (15 cm), slowly spreading and eye catching.

Adiantum hispidulum

Rosy maidenhair, rough maidenhair

TYPE AND SIZE Deciduous, apogamous, 12–18 inches (30–45 cm) tall

HARDINESS Zones 8 (with winter protection) to 10

DISTINCTIVE FEATURES Rhizome is short-creeping. Stipes are whiskered with stiff hairs; a quick rub between the thumb and a finger easily exposes the fern's "hispid" properties. Blades are the familiar pedate (hand) shape with pointed pinnae and crowded, dark green pinnules that are red in new growth.

ORIGIN AND HABITAT This species has a sweeping range from Australia, New Zealand, and the Pacific Islands, including Hawaiian mountaintops, to India, China, Africa, and the Atlantic Islands. It has also naturalized in the southern United States. In nature, it is quite undemanding and it grows in forests, on road banks, and in partially sunny open bush country.

GARDEN AND DESIGN USES The rosy maidenhair is widely sold as an attractive houseplant and is one of the easiest adiantums. Hardy selections are increasingly available and with their rosy new growth are welcome ornaments outdoors in Zone 8, where they may be smaller but every bit as attractive, to Zones 9 and 10, where they willingly thrive.

Adiantum ×mairisii
Mairis's maidenhair

TYPE AND SIZE Deciduous, 15–18 inches (38–45 cm) tall
HARDINESS Zones 7–10
DISTINCTIVE FEATURES Mairis's hardy maidenhair fern is a bushy bipinnate sterile hybrid between *A. capillus-veneris* and an unknown, presumed tropical maidenhair (probably *A. raddianum* or *A. aethiopicum*). It produces lacy, bright green fronds supported by brittle blackish stipes.
ORIGIN AND HABITAT Discovered ages ago in the British nursery of Mairis and Company and named before 1885.
GARDEN AND DESIGN USES This hybrid rewards gardeners in both hot- and cool-summer climates, with typical hybrid vigor and surprising hardiness (better than either of its likely parents). While it is deciduous, this hybrid holds its fronds well into autumn and spreads about with welcome ease in light moist soil and filtered shade. Mairis's maidenhair is lime tolerant, but does not need it to thrive. Despite its age, it is relatively new to North American cultivation.

Adiantum pedatum
Northern maidenhair, five finger fern

TYPE AND SIZE Deciduous, 18–24 inches (45–60 cm) tall
HARDINESS Zones 3–8
DISTINCTIVE FEATURES Rhizome is short-creeping. Brittle stipes fork into two major branches that curl in an indeterminate circular pattern. Unlike *A. aleuticum*, there is rarely a single fan-shaped pinnule between pinnae segments on the rachis. Another important feature is the continuous semicircular outline of the horizontal blade.
ORIGIN AND HABITAT This North American native is found in moist deciduous woods from the Midwest to the length of the Atlantic Coast.
GARDEN AND DESIGN USES Woodland compost is ideal along with regular water, good drainage, and light shade. Northern maidenhair is one of the most familiar, desirable, and ornamental of East Coast fern species evoking woodland beauty and peace. It does not do as well in areas with cool summers. Observant growers on both coasts have found that *A. pedatum* emerges a week or two before *A. aleuticum* and correspondingly disappears earlier in autumn.
SELECTIONS
'Miss Sharples' Deciduous, 15 inches (38 cm), broadly pedate (hand-shaped), luminous lime green, moist shade.

Adiantum venustum

Himalayan maidenhair

TYPE AND SIZE Evergreen or winter green depending on climate, 12–15 inches (30–38 cm) tall
HARDINESS Zones 5 (with protection) to 9
DISTINCTIVE FEATURES The branching rhizome is creeping, eventually supporting a colony of elegant evergreen fronds. The broadly triangular, tripinnate blades emerge in early spring with a flush of salmon-colored frothy feathers and are unaffected by late frosts. Pinnules are typically asymmetrical and conical, somewhat suggestive of mittens.
ORIGIN AND HABITAT This fern is from the forested mountains of Asia, bringing its hardiness and ornamental appeal to woodland gardens throughout the world.
GARDEN AND DESIGN USES Although somewhat slow to establish, A. *venustum* is one of the most desirable additions to any temperate garden, carpeting the shady landscape with softness and reliable light beauty. Because foliage is winter green in Zones 5 and 6 (that is, lasting into but not necessarily through the winter), gardeners should provide winter protection, but all will find it easy to cultivate in moist humus and light shade. Strangely, and regrettably, it does not reproduce willingly from spores. In time, however, most plantings will expand and easily be divided (making impressive gifts). Divisions of an ample size re-establish readily. Small pieces struggle.

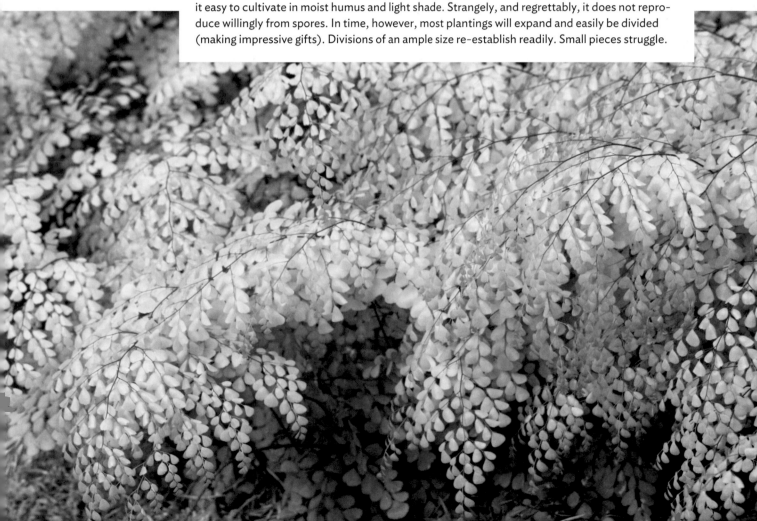

ARACHNIODES

The arachniodes are an elegant and tidy collection of 50 to more than 100 species of evergreens. They share the botanical characteristic of kidney-shaped indusia with *Dryopteris* and the polished, frequently bristle-tipped pinnae and pinnules with *Polystichum*.

The genus name translates from the Greek *arachnion*, spider's web, and *odes*, spiderlike. Legend has it that the herbarium material studied by botanical author Carl Blume (1796–1862) was well wrapped in cobwebs, hence the name. Most arachniodes are from Asia, especially China and Japan. Two species are from the New World.

The rhizomes are short- to long-creeping, supporting a random production of clustered to widely spaced singular fronds. Blades are usually broadly ovate-triangular or pentagonal. Most species are noted for their luster and all those described here are characterized by a greatly elongate lower inner pinnule on the basal pinnae.

Grow this five-star group of ferns in partial sun to shade in light but moist compost.

Arachniodes aristata
Prickly shield fern

TYPE AND SIZE Evergreen, 18–30 inches (45–75 cm) tall
HARDINESS Zones 6–9
DISTINCTIVE FEATURES Rhizome is short- to long-creeping. Brilliant ovate to pentagonal blades that contract abruptly at the tips are tri- to quadripinnate. The innermost pinnules on the lowest pinnae aim downward.
ORIGIN AND HABITAT The native range includes Japan, China, and Korea. The species grows in somewhat dry montane forests.
GARDEN AND DESIGN USES Easily established, *A. aristata* with its classic elegance enhances a lightly shaded bed in woodland duff. Although the rhizome does creep, it produces only a few fronds annually. Use it for a glassy green contrast among subdued soft greens and blues.

Arachniodes simplicior
East Indian holly fern

TYPE AND SIZE Evergreen, 1–2 feet (30–60 cm) tall
HARDINESS Zones 7–9
DISTINCTIVE FEATURES Rhizome is long-creeping, producing fronds periodically. Thick radiant blades are bipinnate daggers with expansive lower pairs of pinnae. In cultivated material, the rachis and pinnae mid-ribs are highlighted with a creamy stripe, one of the few temperate ferns to be variegated.
ORIGIN AND HABITAT Native to the woodlands of China and Japan, this species has escaped (but not invasively) in South Carolina.
GARDEN AND DESIGN USES With its variegation, solid texture, and sparkle, this unique species adds a distinctive elegance in partial shade. Liking heat, it is also comfortable in bright light (not hot midday sun), where it will be more compact. Young growth is unfortunately popu-lar with slugs, but tough mature fronds are resistant. It is occasionally offered under the name *A. aristata* 'Variegata'.

Arachniodes standishii
Upside down fern

TYPE AND SIZE Evergreen, 2–3 feet (60–90 cm) tall

HARDINESS Zones 5–9

DISTINCTIVE FEATURES Rhizome creeps slowly. Broadly ovate blades, produced in a more vase-like arrangement than other arachniodes, are tripinnate-pinnatifid to, rarely, quadripinnate fluff. As is typical for the genus, the innermost lower pinnules on the basal pinnae are enlarged. The sori, when spores are produced at all, ripen annoyingly late in the season.

ORIGIN AND HABITAT *Arachniodes standishii* grows in mountainous forests in Korea and Japan. The Korean material tends to be larger.

GARDEN AND DESIGN USES The long, lacy evergreen fronds arch gracefully over companions in lightly shaded, slightly moist woodlands, making a feathery counterpoint to heavier broadleaf evergreens. The late-ripening spores can be fooled into dropping by picking a fertile pinna, wrapping it securely in white paper, and heating it under the gentle warmth of an incandescent bulb.

ASPLENIUM

Spleenwort

ASpleniums offer a wonderful assortment of fascinating and decorative ferns ranging from elfin and temperamental miniatures to willing rock plants and finally to mammoth tropicals that perch in treetops and adorn living rooms. The genus name is derived from the Greek *a*, without, and *splen*, spleen, and was given by Pliny and Dioscorides because of the fern's reputed ability to cure disorders of the spleen and liver. The approximately 700 species are largely denizens of tropical comforts. By contrast, the temperate species prefer challenging rocky substrates, cliff faces, and associated inhospitable and frequently inaccessible sites.

The usually erect rhizomes have unique translucent latticelike scales. Blades are evergreen and range from simple to finely dissected tripinnate to quadripinnate laciness. Distinctive sori are linear and arranged in a herringbone fashion along veins.

Customized container culture offers promise for growing the temperate species, giving portability to find the ideal site, and a measure of isolation from the ever-present threatening army of slugs. Alternatively, consider decorating the face of a rock wall (as in nature) by plugging crevices with suitable soil, inserting well-rooted plants, and firming them in with moss. Many temperate species are lime lovers, but for safety, it is best to avoid powdered supplements of dolomite or lawn sweeteners. Gypsum can be deadly. Instead, introduce lime via broken small concrete chunks or limestone chips added to the planting hole; these offer a slow release of lime.

Aspleniums rarely produce offshoots for division. They compensate by coming readily and rapidly from spores.

Asplenium fontanum

Fountain spleenwort, smooth rock spleenwort

TYPE AND SIZE Evergreen, 4–8 inches (10–20 cm) tall
HARDINESS Zones 5–8
DISTINCTIVE FEATURES The rhizome is erect. Diminutive lanceolate blades are a lacy, bipinnate-pinnatifid.
ORIGIN AND HABITAT A denizen of dryish, alpine, limestone crevices and walls, this species grows in Europe and the Himalayas.
GARDEN AND DESIGN USES Truly a gem with petite green "fountains" of fronds, the fountain spleenwort is best planted in a trough or alpine house. Loose soil, preferably with a touch of limestone, protection from overwatering, and precautions for eager armies of slugs and snails will help maintain this species at its ornamental best.

Asplenium platyneuron

Ebony spleenwort

TYPE AND SIZE Evergreen, dimorphic, 8–18 inches (20–45 cm) tall
HARDINESS Zones 4–8
DISTINCTIVE FEATURES Rhizome is erect. Pinnae, looking like little wings on the strongly vertical blades, are without stalks and have an auricle (earlike lobe). This species is very close in appearance to *A. resiliens* but differs in having dark reddish brown stipes, rather than black, and having alternate pinnae that usually overlap the rachis.
ORIGIN AND HABITAT This is primarily a midwestern and eastern U.S. native. It grows in basic or slightly acidic soils, on buildings, in woodlands, and in scrub. It prefers light shade.
GARDEN AND DESIGN USES Ebony spleenwort is somewhat difficult to introduce, and the easiest way to acquire this fern may be to buy property where it is already established. It is an attractive, tempting choice for east coast gardens, however, as an unusual dwarf for the foreground, where it will form distinctive colonies when given the right conditions.

Asplenium scolopendrium

Hart's tongue fern
SYNONYM *Phyllitis scolopendrium*

TYPE AND SIZE Evergreen, 1–2 feet (30–60 cm) tall
HARDINESS Zones 4–9
DISTINCTIVE FEATURES Rhizome is erect. Undivided kelly green blades are upright and sturdy, with a heart-shaped base. These are not your stereotypical lacy ferns. Their unfurling shape is credited as being the long-ago pattern for the scrolls on the tips of violin necks. Because of its tongue shape, *A. scolopendrium* was also once considered an herbal antidote to snakebites. The victim was to add a mash of the fern to wine and drink it for relief. A little something to add to your "ten essentials."
ORIGIN AND HABITAT The European species, which is what we traditionally see, along with its myriad varieties in cultivation, grows with abandon often in mortared rubble on antiquities, faces of buildings, and on chinks in roadside walls in Britain, Europe, and beyond. American material is native to limestone habitats in upstate New York, Michigan, and the Bruce Peninsula of Ontario, Canada, and is extremely difficult to cultivate.
GARDEN AND DESIGN USES Hart's tongue selections are almost infinite, but whatever choice makes it to the garden should be cultivated, if possible, in basic soil with that

magic ingredient of good drainage. In his 1908 book, *British Ferns*, Edward Lowe listed 437 cultivars (and apologized for not listing them all). The highest concentrations of commercially available forms, fondly called "scollies," are in groups that are crested, crisped, or have variously altered frond margins as well as combinations thereof. Give the species as well as the varieties a place of honor in the garden's foreground.

SELECTIONS

Crispum Group Wavy undulate and/or frilled margins, with an array of cresting, ranging from the simple forked apex in 'Cristatum' to multiple shredding described by terms such as *digitatum* (fingered) and *ramo* (branched). Heavily crested types such as 'Capitatum' (headed), 'Corymbiferum' (clustered), and 'Grandiceps' (with large terminal crests) have fronds that are simple at their base, but are topped with ornate headdresses. Two cultivars that are extremely popular and are fortunately in commerce are 'Laceratum Kaye', a leaf lettuce of a fern with fringed edges, and 'Peraferens', which in an amazing display of foliar acrobatics has a curled frond apex enclosing a minute extended needle of foliar tissue. Both come true from spores.

Asplenium trichomanes

Maidenhair spleenwort

TYPE AND SIZE Evergreen, 4–8 inches (10–20 cm) tall

HARDINESS Zones 3–9

DISTINCTIVE FEATURES Rhizome is ascending. Stipes on some varieties may persist for years as upright, naked spikes. Narrow, once-pinnate blades are linear with pairs of round to oblong petite pinnae. *Asplenium trichomanes* is a botanically complex species with chromosome numbers, ecology, and to a certain extent morphology factoring in identification. Subspecies and proposed subspecies recently numbered twenty. The most recognized are subsp. *trichomanes*, with a strong preference for acidic habitats, and subsp. *quadrivalens*, a lime lover adorning fissures in castle walls and antiquities in the United Kingdom and Europe.

ORIGIN AND HABITAT The maidenhair spleenwort is a circumpolar cosmopolitan with populations on every continent except Antarctica.

GARDEN AND DESIGN USES This is one of the finest miniature ferns for the garden community. Slugs ignore it, and the tidy presentation makes it ideal for grouping in the garden's foreground. For a special display, treat it as a solo artist in a container. Plant it in light shade to partial sun and a coarsely mixed soil. The assorted attractive cultivars are equally adaptable and come true from spores.

SELECTIONS

'Cristatum' Crested frond tips.

'Incisum' Pinnule margins deeply cut.

'Plumosum' Ruffled foliage.

ASTROLEPIS

Until relatively recently, the six to eight *Astrolepis* (star-scaled cloak fern) species were classified with fellow drylanders *Cheilanthes* and/or *Notholaena*. The name is derived from the Greek *astro*, star, and *lepis*, scale.

Astrolepis sinuata

TYPE AND SIZE Evergreen, 18 inches (45 cm) tall

HARDINESS Zones 7–9

DISTINCTIVE FEATURES This stunning fern has furry, bluish, upright, pinnate blades. The upper pinnae surfaces have a smattering of protective starry hairs, and the lower surfaces are crowded with a thick mat of matching silver to tan scales. The margins do not have inrolled pinnae.

ORIGIN AND HABITAT An exclusively New World native accustomed to sunny desert locales with periodic summer monsoons but dry winters.

GARDEN AND DESIGN USES Best in part sun; frame it with rocks. In cultivation, this fetching novelty needs well-drained, gravelly soil, and a site offering winter wet protection (under overhanging eaves or featured in a specialized alpine house). It is not as temperamental as some of the other xerics.

ATHYRIUM

Lady fern

Athyriums are cold-hardy Northern Hemisphere ferns, with a few freeze-tolerant strays from South America. Many of the truly ornamental athyriums are introductions from fern-rich Asia. These imports offer a delightful array of subtle to remarkable foliar color and forms.

There is no official derivation for the name *Athyrium*. However, the Greek *athoros* means good at breeding, which is certainly apropos for the lady ferns and may even be considered an understatement.

Worldwide there are approximately 200 species. Almost all are deciduous. The North American natives adjust to sites with varying degrees of shade to moist, sun-drenched locales. Stout, sometimes branching, rhizomes are erect to long-creeping. Blades range from short to tall and modestly pinnate to sumptuously quadripinnate.

The fronds lack the strengthening tissue of other fern genera and consequently are easily snapped. The planting site should be chosen accordingly—away from cruising dogs, feisty squirrels, and wayward watering systems. Some species produce fresh fronds throughout the season, and some can look tattered by mid-summer. All appreciate moist, neutral to acidic soil.

Propagation is problem-free. Spores germinate readily (sometimes far too freely). Division, for those species with branching rhizomes, is strictly a matter of timing and a sharp knife. While the species generally breed uniformly from spores, most of the cultivars need to be propagated by division or tissue culture to retain their unique characteristics.

Athyrium filix-femina
Lady fern

TYPE AND SIZE Deciduous, 3–6 feet (0.9–1.8 m) tall

HARDINESS Zones 4–8

DISTINCTIVE FEATURES Rhizome is stout and erect. Lanceolate blades are bipinnate-pinnatifid. At one time nearly 300 cultivars were associated with this species. (Please note that *filix* is not spelled *felix* [= happy].)

ORIGIN AND HABITAT *Athyrium filix-femina* is found practically worldwide, growing primarily in moist to wet acidic sites in shade or sun.

GARDEN AND DESIGN USES These adaptable ferns are easily cultivated and may often volunteer. Native eastern U.S. varieties are somewhat better mannered and useful in gardens, including those of the hot and humid interior. The common name is from ancient Greek tradition where this fern was considered the female, lacier, counterpart to the robust male fern, *Dryopteris filix-mas*. (This overlooks the fact that the lady is often considerably taller.)

SELECTIONS

Cristatum Group ▼ Crested frond tips and pinnae.

Athyrium filix-femina
(continued)

'Dre's Dagger' Compact crisscrossed pinnae form letter X. Cruciatocristatum Group.
'Frizelliae' ▶ Tatting fern with tiny round beadlike pinnae, new growth late.
'Lady in Red' ▲ A superior selection. It has glassy ruby stipes balancing attractively with the lime-green foliage. Note that the luminescent color, which is more pronounced with some sun, does not fully develop until after at least one cold winter. For brightest color, refrain from fertilizing.

'Minutissimum' ▲ True plant is a miniature copy of the species that matures at 6 inches (15 cm). Many imposters are larger.

'Vernoniae' ▲ Maroon stipes and crisped pinnae margins.
'Victoriae' ◄ Crisscrossed fringed pinnae form letter X.

Athyrium niponicum

TYPE AND SIZE Deciduous, 1–2 feet (30–60 cm) tall
HARDINESS Zones 4–9
DISTINCTIVE FEATURES Rhizome is short- to long-creeping and branching. Stipes are a pronounced burgundy color. The soft green bipinnate to bipinnate-pinnatifid blade is narrowly ovate. (Please note *niponicum* has only one *p*.)
ORIGIN AND HABITAT This species is from the ferny triumvirate of Japan, Korea, and China, where it is a common woodlander.

GARDEN AND DESIGN USES Far better known for its 'Pictum' showpieces, this species, with its subtle, soft patina of pastel greens, but no silver, wears quietly well in the garden. Pair it with forest green leafage in evenly moist part shade.
SELECTIONS AND HYBRIDS
'Applecourt' ▼ A selection of the species with crested and colorful fronds to 2 feet (60 cm), colonizes slowly.
'Burgundy Lace' Strong accents of deep burgundy to purple on silver. Low growing.

'Pictum' ▼ Among the many choices, the popular and incredibly variable Japanese painted fern, *Athyrium niponicum* 'Pictum', is one of the most universally recognized and functional of all garden-worthy ferns. This outstanding and deservedly popular fern has deciduous blades that are silvery with an infusion of burgundy. It can be cultivated with confidence and color in all areas of North America from San Diego, through the hot and humid interior sectors, to the cold of eastern Canada. Height and coloration are variable, but all are welcome in loose, evenly moist, neutral soil and light shade, without direct sun. Fresh fronds offer added enjoyment throughout the summer. This cultivar was honored as the North American Perennial Plant Association's Plant of the Year for 2004, the first fern to be so recognized.

'Regal Red' A slow spreader with central highlights of bright red to burgundy wrapped in silver and green. Holds its 8- to 20-inch (20- to 50-cm) fronds well into autumn.

'Silver Falls' ▼ Aptly named selection with arching, 12-inch (30-cm) predominantly silver fronds.

Athyrium niponicum
(continued)

***Athyrium* 'Branford Beauty'** ▼ Deciduous. Carries colorful upright 12- to 30-inch (30- to 75-cm) fronds, showing its painted heritage. A presumed hybrid of *A. niponicum* 'Pictum' and *A. filix-femina*. Zones 4–8.
***Athyrium* 'Branford Rambler'** ▶ Deciduous. Long-creeping and colorful, but with predominantly green fronds; 12–24 inches (30–60 cm). A presumed hybrid of *A. niponicum* 'Pictum' and *A. filix-femina*. Zones 4–8.

***Athyrium* 'Ghost'** ▲ Deciduous. A prize with a bushy vertical display of steely gray (ghostly) swords to 3 feet (90 cm) and a stunning insert amid dark green foliage in light to full shade. A presumed hybrid of *A. niponicum* 'Pictum' and *A. filix-femina*. Zones 3–8.

***Athyrium* 'Ocean's Fury'** ◄ Deciduous. Silver, to 3 feet (90 cm) tall and wide, with delicate crests on frond and pinnae tips. A presumed hybrid of *A. niponicum* 'Pictum' and *A. filix-femina*. Zones 3–8.

Athyrium otophorum

Eared lady fern, auriculate lady fern

TYPE AND SIZE Evergreen to deciduous, 1.5–2 feet (45–90 cm) tall

HARDINESS Zones 6–9

DISTINCTIVE FEATURES Rhizome is erect. Stipes are dark burgundy. Bipinnate triangular blades are matte green, suffused with maroon. It is significant that the pinnae on the species are not stalked. The pinnules are lobed and have a thumblike auricle, the ear of the common name, adjacent to the rachis. Variety *okanum* with stalked pinnae is commonly available and more frequently cultivated than the type.

ORIGIN AND HABITAT This is a colorful fern of woodlands in Japan, Korea, and China.

GARDEN AND DESIGN USES Like the Japanese painted fern, this species flourishes in North American climates. In the punishing winter extremes of the northeastern United States, however, heavy mulching encourages survival, and growers have reported it is easier to establish plantings in the spring. New growth with distinctive lime and burgundy foliage unfurls early in the season in the Pacific Northwest, but late in the eastern United States. As the fronds age, the lime softens to a more subdued grayish green patina (gray being a distinguishing feature of maturity). Eared lady fern is an excellent choice for adding vitality to shaded woodlands away from direct sunlight. As a bonus, plants will hold their fronds throughout mild winters (occasional dips to 28°F/−2°C and up). Even in colder climates, this species maintains its fronds in picturesque condition well into cold weather.

BLECHNUM
Deer fern

Blechnums are colorful species that rejoice in humid-rich environments and excel in moist to spongy acidic soil. They are shade-loving plants of forest floors, road banks, and mountainsides, often carpeting their native habitats with showy, rosy, luminous foliage. They are welcome accents in both garden and home.

The genus name is derived from the Greek *blechnon*, an ancient name for fern. The world's 180 to 200 species are concentrated in the Southern Hemisphere, with New Zealand, Chilean, and Australian natives offering a potpourri of hardy and potentially hardy species of horticultural interest.

Structurally this is a uniform group, with evergreen, pinnatifid to pinnate blades. Rhizomes are usually erect or occasionally creeping, and in some species may form a modest trunk. Most but not all species are dimorphic (having two types of fronds: fertile and sterile). The sterile fronds are low evergreen rosettes, whereas the fertile are boldly upright deciduous stalks with linear pinnae enclosing the spores.

Propagation from spores is an inconsistent science. All species should be sown as soon as practicable after the spores mature. Those producing creeping rhizomes are easily divided.

Though only a few qualify as cold hardy, those that do are an elite addition to moisture-nourished woodlands, where they offer a tidy year-round presence and are strongly recommended for their refreshing visual enrichment.

Blechnum chilense

TYPE AND SIZE Evergreen, dimorphic, 3–5 feet (0.9–1.5 m) tall

HARDINESS Zones 7 (with protection) to 9

DISTINCTIVE FEATURES Rhizome is long-creeping, tossing up sturdy erect fronds at random. The once-pinnate, narrowly oblong blades carry pairs of rubbery pinnae on a bit of a stalk. The extended apex resembles an elongated pinna. The lower edges of the pinnae overlap the rachis. This characteristic is one of the few distinctions between this species and the extremely closely related *B. cordatum*.

ORIGIN AND HABITAT *Blechnum chilense* is abundant in Chile and also grows in Argentina, Brazil, and Uruguay. In the lowlands, the new growth is green, but at higher elevations, the new fronds can be a fetching red. This species is a common and sensational ornamental in the botanical gardens of the British Isles and, with its increasing availability, is immensely popular in the United States.

GARDEN AND DESIGN USES Here is an excellent choice for instant impact in moisture and part shade. Surprisingly it will tolerate dry shade, but the growth is much slower and the fronds are rarely over 2 feet (60 cm) long. The huge (by ferny standards) fronds are frequently enhanced by bright red new growth, especially in nutrient-poor soils, and give an exuberant tropical magnificence to temperate gardens. Chileans call the unfurling frond with inrolled pinnae *costillas de la vaca*, ribs of the cow. This species, with its long rhizomes, is tailor-made for division. Propagators and growers should take care, however, and not apply fertilizer to very young plants. Sturdy, established plants are not affected, but with their natural vigor do not need any supplemental food.

Blechnum discolor
Crown fern

TYPE AND SIZE Evergreen, 1.5–3 feet (45–90 cm) tall
HARDINESS Zones 8 (with protection) to 10
DISTINCTIVE FEATURES Rhizome is erect, rather quickly forming a trunk of 6–12 inches (15–30 cm). The blades are a bright green with whitish undersides. Fountains of fertile fronds flow from the center of the sterile rosettes and are an intriguing combination of sterile and fertile pinnae, with the lower portions zigzag stubs of sterile tissue and the upper portions pointed darts of sori.
ORIGIN AND HABITAT This species is endemic to New Zealand, where it is abundant in damp to dry soil in beech forests especially at higher elevations and on the North Island. In native habitats, the stolons wander about producing magnificent colonies of foliage.
GARDEN AND DESIGN USES *Blechnum discolor* is easily identified by the lightness of the frond underside, which makes it ideal for hanging or posting up where the "discolor" can be admired. (The Māori use these fronds with their white undersides as trail markers.) Give it light soil and partial shade. The spores are short lived and must be sown as soon as ripe.

Blechnum fluviatile
Ray water fern, creek fern

TYPE AND SIZE Evergreen, dimorphic, 12–18 inches (30–45 cm) tall
HARDINESS Zones 8–9
DISTINCTIVE FEATURES Rhizome is erect. Ground-hugging sterile fronds radiate horizontally with oval 0.4-inch (9-mm) pinnae trimmed in dark bristles. The fertile fronds are strongly upright.
ORIGIN AND HABITAT This wonderful little specimen is native to New Zealand and Australia in dampish surroundings.
GARDEN AND DESIGN USES Grow *B. fluviatile*, with its attractive procumbent pinwheel presentation, in moist and protected shadelands, where it will gently colonize and certainly please the viewer.

Blechnum niponicum

Japanese deer fern

TYPE AND SIZE Evergreen, dimorphic, 12–18 inches (30–45 cm) tall

HARDINESS Zones 6–9

DISTINCTIVE FEATURES Rhizome is erect. This species balances prostrate 12- to 18-inch-wide (30–45 cm) rosettes of evergreen sterile, once-pinnate fronds and upright, deciduous, fertile spikes of equal length.

ORIGIN AND HABITAT This is a fern of mountainous forests in China, Japan, and Korea.

GARDEN AND DESIGN USES This choice tidy species displays with elegant restraint in the peat-enriched foreground of lightly shaded woodlands. New growth is brilliant pink. Once established, expect a dependable year-round display of sturdy low-growing fronds.

Blechnum novae-zelandiae
Palm leaf fern

TYPE AND SIZE Evergreen, dimorphic, 2–5 feet (60–150 cm) tall

HARDINESS Zones 7–9

DISTINCTIVE FEATURES Rhizome is short-creeping, producing dense clusters of frond bouquets. Fronds with oval, once-pinnate sterile blades offer showers of bright pinnae with wavy margins.

ORIGIN AND HABITAT This species is a common fern in New Zealand, where it is found in moist, shady woodlands.

GARDEN AND DESIGN USES With variously shaded glossy green-hued foliage, this species offers a showy enrichment. Well-irrigated, wet loamy soil and light shade are the keys to success. Although the species may reach 5 feet in its natural habitats, it favors the lower dimension in cultivation.

Blechnum penna-marina

Alpine water fern, little hard fern

TYPE AND SIZE Evergreen, dimorphic, 4–12 inches (10–30 cm) tall

HARDINESS Zones 6–8

DISTINCTIVE FEATURES Rhizome is short-creeping, producing tight clusters of prostrate sterile fronds and upright fertile spikes. The once-pinnate, 0.5-inch-wide (13 mm) blades emerge in brilliant russet tones. There is also a crested form.

ORIGIN AND HABITAT *Blechnum penna-marina* is as varied in its native habitats as it is accommodating in cultivation. Its range extends from wet lowlands to alpine talus in New Zealand and Australia, with related colonies in South America. The South American material is generally larger and has minimal russet tones on the new growth.

GARDEN AND DESIGN USES With its small stature and adaptability, this is a marvelous fern as a groundcover. In cool sites, it is an excellent choice for sun, where it remains tidily compact and colorful throughout the seasons. In hot climates, it needs protection from intense midday sunshine. It can become raggedy and a tad too rambunctious in too much shade. Alpine water fern prefers acidic, well-drained moist soils. Like many creeping ferns, and blechnums in particular, it does not propagate readily from spores. However, with its crawling rhizomes, division is easy.

Blechnum spicant
Deer fern

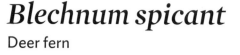

TYPE AND SIZE Evergreen, dimorphic, 18–30 inches (45–75 cm) tall
HARDINESS Zones 5–8
DISTINCTIVE FEATURES Rhizome is erect. Evergreen, oblanceolate, sterile fronds are once-pinnate and arranged in whorls of three or more growing horizontally at the same level around a stem. Deciduous fertile fronds are taller and upright.
ORIGIN AND HABITAT This jewel of the woodlands can be found in acidic soil in deep to light shade in the coniferous forests of the Pacific Northwest and sweeping down gullies in wet acidic seeps in Europe.
GARDEN AND DESIGN USES The deer fern is an extremely well man-nered and welcome addition to soft, peat-enriched soil in moist shade. With its coniferous forest background, it is a natural companion plant for woodland spring ephemerals, where the combination produces a handsome portrait to welcome a long-awaited spring. The deer fern is, however, totally intolerant of lime—whether applied inadvertently in a general broadcast of an all-purpose fertilizer or as an inherent ingredi-ent of native soils or water—so do site it accordingly.
SELECTIONS
'Cristatum' ▼ Bears fronds with crests at the apex.
'Rickard's Serrate' ◄ Neatly scalloped pinnae margins.

CHEILANTHES
Lip fern

As dryland ferns, cheilanthes are quite the opposite of stereotypical woodland shade lovers. In severe drought, the entire plant can curl without damaging its cell structure, only to rehydrate when given water, a characteristic that has earned some of them the epithet resurrection fern.

The genus name comes from the Greek *cheilos*, lip, and *anthos*, flower, referring to the curled pinnae margins that enclose the sori. The 180 to 200 species are distributed worldwide, with concentrations in the American Southwest and Mexico. Most species are short and strongly vertical with blades often very finely divided, up to quadripinnate. Diagnostic cottony hairs and/or woolly scales moderate the ambient temperature around the fronds, reflect heat and light, and catch dew and any available moisture.

Many avid gardeners attempt these ferns for their unique ornamental qualities as well as the challenge of establishing notoriously difficult species. Some plants are very soil specific. All require free-draining soil with added volcanic rock, pumice, and/or granite grit. (It is extremely important to wash these inorganic additives first to flush away the siltlike fines that can clog oxygen circulation in the soil.) Add composted bark, charcoal, and humus to the basic mix. Tall narrow pots provide the best drainage for containerized plants.

These xerics need good air circulation, bright light, and protection from winter wet. In hot climates, light shade is appropriate. In cool, cloudy climates, full sun, at least in winter, is suitable.

Propagation can be accomplished by removing small rooted pieces from the perimeter of the fern or by sowing spores. Some species are apogamous, producing new plants without sexual fertilization.

Cheilanthes eatonii

Eaton's lip fern

TYPE AND SIZE Evergreen, 15 inches (38 cm) tall
HARDINESS Zones 7–10
DISTINCTIVE FEATURES Rhizome is short-creeping.
Stipes are brown. The blade is lanceolate and covered
with whitish hairs above and creamy hairs and scales
below. This choice, extremely handsome, tufted xeric
is easier to grow than most of its kin but still requires
devoted care.
ORIGIN AND HABITAT *Cheilanthes eatonii* grows across
the southwestern United States in various substrates.
GARDEN AND DESIGN USES This dryland fern needs sun
and good drainage.

Cheilanthes fendleri

Fendler's lip fern

TYPE AND SIZE Evergreen, 1 foot (30 cm) tall
HARDINESS Zones 6–10
DISTINCTIVE FEATURES Rhizome is long-creeping, forming colonies as it wanders. Stipes are dark brown. The lower
side of the green blade is covered with white to rusty brown
scales. A distinguishing feature is the absence of hairs on
the tips of the scales.
ORIGIN AND HABITAT This species grows in various substrates from Colorado south to northern Mexico.
GARDEN AND DESIGN USES Give this xeric fern sun and
good drainage, and protection from winter wet. This species is one of the easier-to-grow members of the genus.

Cheilanthes lindheimeri
Fairy swords

TYPE AND SIZE Evergreen, apogamous, 8–12 inches (20–30 cm) tall

HARDINESS Zones 7–9

DISTINCTIVE FEATURES Rhizome is long-creeping. Stipes are woolly. Quadripinnate upright fronds are a vision of white curly hairs.

ORIGIN AND HABITAT This species colonizes along the edges of igneous rocks, sandstone, and granite in the American Southwest.

GARDEN AND DESIGN USES Grow this striking treasure in exposed rocky sites with gritty soil, good drainage, and minimum winter wet.

Cheilanthes tomentosa
Woolly lip fern

TYPE AND SIZE Evergreen, apogamous, 8–15 inches (20–38 cm) tall

HARDINESS Zones 7–9

DISTINCTIVE FEATURES Rhizome is short-creeping, producing dense colonies of gray green fronds. The russet stipes have creamy hairs, giving them a pinkish hue. Blades are oblong-lanceolate and tripinnate. The upper surface is lightly trimmed with spidery white hairs, and the lower surface has a combination of whitish hairs and scales.

ORIGIN AND HABITAT This is a species of the American Mid to Southwest, where it grows on rocks in various soil types from basic to acidic.

GARDEN AND DESIGN USES The woolly lip fern is one of the easiest xerics to establish in gardens. It is happiest in a fast-draining soil mix of pumice, bark, charcoal, and humus. For those eager to cultivate xeric ferns, this is a litmus plant. With good luck, proceed.

CONIOGRAMME
Bamboo fern

Coniogramme is a little-known increasingly popular genus that includes a collection of species with a nontraditional profile. Rather than feathery plumes, these have willowy elongate pinnae suggestive of bamboo leaves.

There are upwards of 20 species worldwide, most of them in Africa, eastern Asia, and the Pacific Rim. The genus name is derived from *conio*, dusky, and *gramme*, line, in reference to the arrangement of the sori.

The typical species has a short-creeping rhizome and upright fronds. Only a few temperate species are in cultivation. *Coniogramme japonica*, the species most common in western horticulture, captures the bamboo look of the common name.

Coniogramme emeiensis
Chinese bamboo fern

TYPE AND SIZE Deciduous, 2–3 feet (60–90 cm) tall
HARDINESS Zones 8–10
DISTINCTIVE FEATURES A unique conversation piece with bipinnate fronds that are mildly and handsomely variegated in a laddered herringbone pattern. Vein configuration is free (not netted).
ORIGIN AND HABITAT This bamboo fern comes from Mount Emei (Omei) in China, where it grows in the nutrient-rich forest floor.
GARDEN AND DESIGN USES The green willowy foliage with creamy veins maintains best coloring in partial shade.

Coniogramme intermedia
Intermediate bamboo fern

TYPE AND SIZE Semievergreen, 2–4 feet (60–120 cm) tall

HARDINESS Zones 7–10

DISTINCTIVE FEATURES Tall stipes support bipinnate blades with long linear pinnae. It is significant that the veins are free and forked.

ORIGIN AND HABITAT Intermediate bamboo fern grows in the forests of eastern Asia including the Himalayas.

GARDEN AND DESIGN USES Like all forest-dwellers, intermediate bamboo fern needs moist, rich soil in deep shade to look its best. It provides an interesting contrast with finely textured plants.

SELECTIONS

'Rasha' 18 inches (45 cm), totally different contorted linear fronds.

'Shishi' ▶ 2 feet (60 cm), dark green glossy fringed pinnae, spreads slowly.

'Yoroi Musha' ▼ 3 feet (90 cm), irregularly shaped dark fronds present an eye-catching showstopper, creeps just a bit.

CYATHEA

Tree ferns are marvels of the plant kingdom, having once dominated the world's landscape. Their fossil records go back some 300 million years, and *Cyathea*, at about 144 million years, is a relative newcomer. Its approximately 600 species are solid members of the humid, mountainous subtropics, with scaly trunks to 8 inches (20 cm) in diameter. Fronds with long stipes grow up to 18 feet (5.4 m), and young trunks may grow as much as 1 foot (30 cm) a year. The genus name is from the Greek *kyathos*, wine cup, referring to the indusia that circle the sori on the undersides of the fronds. (In contrast, *Dicksonia* has sori on its margins and hairs on its trunks.)

A few species are amenable to cultivation in temperate zones. Plant them in moist, lime-free soil and protect them from wind. The trunks, which house the roots externally, should be watered copiously until they are established. Do not water the crowns in winter in cold climates. Instead, stuff them with straw to protect the tip from freezing. Enthusiasts put the whole plant to bed well mulched and wrapped in foam, covered bubble wrap, straw, aluminum foil, and fleece or combinations thereof. Plants with trunks of 2 feet (60 cm) or more are less cold susceptible.

Propagation is from spores, but many species are rooted from loglike cuttings of the trunks sunk in moist soil. It takes quite some time, and they need to be supported and kept moist throughout the process.

Cyathea cooperi

Australian tree fern, coin spot tree fern
SYNONYMS *Sphaeropteris cooperi, Alsophila cooperi*

TYPE AND SIZE Evergreen, 40 feet (12 m) tall
HARDINESS Zones 8 (with heavy winter protection) to 10
DISTINCTIVE FEATURES The trunk can quickly reach 40 feet (12 m) and has coin spots, oval scars where old fronds have broken away. Bipinnate-pinnatifid broadly lanceolate fronds on long stipes arch to 15 feet (4.5 m). Stipes and trunk have white scales with brownish teeth.
ORIGIN AND HABITAT This species is endemic to Australia, where it grows in rain forests up to 4500 feet (1400 m). It has escaped in the Hawaiian Islands and is a serious environmental threat to their native tree fern populations.
GARDEN AND DESIGN USES The Australian tree fern is one of the most widely grown and popular tree ferns for cultivation in the continental United States, growing quickly in humid and moist sites. It takes brief exposure to light frost, but must be enclosed in a protective wrap where winter cold is common.

Cyathea dealbata
Silver fern

TYPE AND SIZE Evergreen, 30 feet (9 m) tall

HARDINESS Zones 9–10

DISTINCTIVE FEATURES The trunk, with protruding persistent stipe bases, grows slowly to 30 feet (9 m). Bipinnate-pinnatifid lanceolate fronds extend to 12 feet (3.6 m). They are pale green on the upper surface and the mature plants are coated with showy silver powder on the undersides.

ORIGIN AND HABITAT This New Zealand endemic grows in well-drained soil at elevations up to 3000 feet (900 m).

GARDEN AND DESIGN USES According to George Schenk, this plant is known in Kiwi English as silver fern and in Māori as *ponga*, and it is one of the slowest tree ferns to develop arboreally.

Cyathea medullaris
Black tree fern

TYPE AND SIZE Evergreen, 60 feet (18 m) tall
HARDINESS Zones 9–10
DISTINCTIVE FEATURES The black trunk, which is covered with scars from fallen fronds, grows rather quickly to 60 feet (18 m) in the wild. At a slender 8 inches (20 cm) in diameter, the trunk supports bipinnate-pinnatifid to tripinnate masses of fronds 10–18 feet (3–5.4 m) long on a black skeleton with black scales.
ORIGIN AND HABITAT This native of the South Pacific grows in dark gullies at elevations up to 1500 feet (450 m).
GARDEN AND DESIGN USES Although a striking tree fern, it is rarely available for cultivation outside of its native range. However, it has recently been imported into England, where it does best in frost-free environs.

Cyathea smithii
Soft tree fern

TYPE AND SIZE Evergreen, 25 feet (7.5 m) tall
HARDINESS Zones 9–10
DISTINCTIVE FEATURES The brown trunk reaches 25 feet (7.5 m) and is surrounded just below the crown by skirts of dead frond midribs that offer protective insulation from winter cold. Soft green, tripinnate fronds are 7 to 9 feet (2.1–2.7 m) long and have abundant brown scales along the stipes.
ORIGIN AND HABITAT This species, the most southerly growing of the world's tree ferns, is native to high elevations in New Zealand and as far south as the Auckland Islands. It prefers wet cold forests and thrives right up to the snow line of the glaciers on New Zealand's South Island.
GARDEN AND DESIGN USES Like most tree ferns, it needs humus-rich soil plus shelter from wind and cold winters.

CYRTOMIUM
Holly fern

Cyrtomiums are commonly called holly ferns due to the resemblance, given a little imagination, of the pinnae to holly leaves. Their numbers are few by fern standards, about 20 species, and their distribution is equally restricted, with all but one species native to Asia (although two species have naturalized in the United States). By contrast, options for ornamental applications—from the garden to the shaded shelf by the kitchen window—are far from confined. The distinctive, atypical fern foliage serves graciously as a contrast for delicate companions and, with their leathery constitution, several adapt to less-than-fern-friendly indoor habitats.

The fronds are evergreen or subevergreen (evergreen in mild but not cold winters). Many are finished in soft matte patinas of light yellow or grayish green. Blades are pinnate with an abundance of peltate (centrally attached) sori scattered randomly on the undersides. The stipes are proportionately short. The genus name comes from the Greek *kyrtoma*, arched, referring to the arching appearance of the netted veins that are one of the signature characteristics of the genus.

Cyrtomiums are easily cultivated and one of the best options for, but not confined to, deep shade. Plant them in a fern mix of light compost-rich duff. Some species are from limestone habitats, but limey supplements are not necessary.

Spore propagation is very efficient and yields crops quickly (sometimes even when not expected). Division is generally not an option, as the species rarely produce multiple crowns. Some species are apogamous, producing new plants without sexual fertilization.

Cyrtomium falcatum
Japanese holly fern, Asian holly fern

TYPE AND SIZE Evergreen, apogamous, 1–2 feet (30–60 cm) tall
HARDINESS Zones 7–10
DISTINCTIVE FEATURES Rhizome is erect. Rosettes of once-pinnate, oblong blades are a unique lacquered forest green. Fronds are whorled (three or more growing at the same level around a stem).
ORIGIN AND HABITAT This species grows in lowland regions in Japan, China, Taiwan, Korea, India, and Vietnam. It has escaped and naturalized in many areas of the world.
GARDEN AND DESIGN USES With its whorls of shiny green fronds, Japanese holly fern is an easy and outstanding accent plant, especially when surrounded by contrasting gossamer foliage. Give it average fern soil and light to dark shade, as it will burn in too much sun. Its leathery texture makes it an ideal candidate, together with its varieties, for indoor use.
SELECTIONS
'Butterfieldii' ▶ Glossy fringed pinnae, ornamental indoors or out, shade.

Cyrtomium fortunei
Fortune's holly fern

TYPE AND SIZE Evergreen, apogamous, 30 inches (75 cm) tall

HARDINESS Zones 5–10

DISTINCTIVE FEATURES Rhizome is erect. Fronds arching and upright, with lanceolate, once-pinnate, lightly luminous blades. Pinnae with a matching terminal pinna are oblong and sometimes bear prominent thumbs. Variety *intermedium* and variety *clivicola* produce low rosettes of lime-green pinnae.

ORIGIN AND HABITAT This is a fern of Korea, China, Vietnam, and Thailand, and it is especially common in Japan, where it grows from city walls to mountainous forest floors. Like *Cyrtomium falcatum*, it has escaped in a disjunct assortment of habitats.

GARDEN AND DESIGN USES This is the *Cyrtomium* species for Zone 5 or 6 climates with cold winters and successfully survives rigorous temperature extremes. Woodland compost and light to deep shade will maintain a healthy display of soft green fronds.

Cyrtomium lonchitoides

TYPE AND SIZE Evergreen, 12–18 inches (30–45 cm) tall

HARDINESS Zones 6–9

DISTINCTIVE FEATURES Rhizome is erect. Compact upright blades are once-pinnate with pale green pinnae.

ORIGIN AND HABITAT This holly fern is endemic to the woodlands of China.

GARDEN AND DESIGN USES With its small stature and unusual profile, this species is an attractive and versatile foreground feature in full shade with woodland perennials.

Cyrtomium macrophyllum

Large-leafed holly fern

TYPE AND SIZE Evergreen, apogamous, 1–2 feet (30–60 cm) tall

HARDINESS Zones 6–10

DISTINCTIVE FEATURES Rhizome is erect, producing a frugal rosette of unfernlike, portly pinnae. Lanceolate blades are once-pinnate with broad pinnae surrounding a large (macro) terminal pinna.

ORIGIN AND HABITAT According to *Flora of Japan*, the species grows in dense, gloomy forests. With its pale mats of foliar lightness, perhaps this is nature's way of brightening the gloom. It is also found in the Himalayas and China.

GARDEN AND DESIGN USES This species settles into the shaded glens of woodland gardens, where with its nontraditional outline and matte green fronds, it is a welcome contrast to frilly and dark foliage.

CYSTOPTERIS

Bladder fern

Bladder ferns spread deciduous, small, and sometimes inconspicuous colonies throughout cool sites in mountainous areas worldwide. Their delicate fronds are among the first, along with the woodsias, to unfurl in late winter. Consequently, their fertility is precocious and the fronds often wither early in the summer, having accomplished a quick and efficient cycle of growth.

Fronds range in height from 8 to 24 inches (20–60 cm) and are from once-pinnate to tripinnate. Sori are covered by a bladderlike membrane. This early deciduous membrane is soon gone, however, often making identification confusing. Ripe spores are black. (Woodsias, while sometimes similar in appearance, produce brown spores.)

The genus name comes from the Greek *kystis*, bladder, referring to the appearance of the swollen membrane covering the sori, and the universally applied *pteris*, fern. Worldwide, there are approximately 20 species. They are easily grown in moist to wet, often highly basic, friable soil or rock crevices in temperate gardens. Their deciduous cold winter rest is mandatory.

Propagation by either division or spores (which ripen very early) is easily accomplished. For *Cystopteris bulbifera* and its hybrid offspring, with their abundant supplies of pealike rolling bulblets, reproduction frequently occurs without any attention, or even awareness, from the grower. Surprises happen.

Cystopteris bulbifera
Bulblet bladder fern

TYPE AND SIZE Deciduous, 18–30 inches (45–75 cm) tall
HARDINESS Zones 3–8
DISTINCTIVE FEATURES Rhizome is short-creeping. Clear wine red stipes are a refreshing spring tonic. Bipinnate blades, with lime-green foliage, are elongate, usually downward draping, triangular spears of pinnae. The foliage often has an undercoat of three or more minute bulblets. Unlike most fern bulbils, these fall readily and spread cascading colonies of plantlets. As these are easily plucked, they are not an invasive threat.
ORIGIN AND HABITAT This species is distributed from midwestern to eastern North America. In nature, it grows primarily on limestone. Look (up) for it on ledges where bulbil-encouraged rivulets of the fern flow down in moisture-rich crevices.

GARDEN AND DESIGN USES The most unique of the bladder ferns, this species needs shade. A limestone substrate encourages good health but is not necessary for survival. Let it flow through consistently moist sites, where it will produce a continuous fountain of foliage and willingly populate surrounding garden sites with its bulblet castoffs. There is a crested as well as a "crispa" variety.

Cystopteris fragilis
Fragile fern

TYPE AND SIZE Deciduous, 8–16 inches (20–40 cm) tall
HARDINESS Zones 2–9
DISTINCTIVE FEATURES Rhizome is short-creeping, bearing food-storing stubs of old stipes. Lanceolate blades are bipinnate, with thin-textured lax pinnae. The new fronds unfurl early and eagerly in spring. On the downside, they often collapse (or at least look weary) soon after dispersing their spores in early summer.
ORIGIN AND HABITAT This is one of the most common of the world's ferns, with populations distributed in cool mountainous habitats from the Siberian cold to the high-elevation tropics. Plants prefer damp sites within the rocky chinks of a lime substrate.
GARDEN AND DESIGN USES This species is easily cultivated and, although it will adapt almost anywhere, it likes being cold and nestled into limestone crumble. Unfortunately, fragile ferns tend to be lacking in dynamics and are best used as fillers where other, more ornamental options have not succeeded. Watch for slugs.

DENNSTAEDTIA

This is a genus of strong—some might say strongly aggressive—species with soft, feathery deciduous fronds. Most of the approximately 55 species are native to the subtropics or tropics, but a few are temperate and useful in their ready adaptability. They have short to widely creeping rhizomes. Pale fronds are broad at the base and pinnate-pinnatifid to tripinnate. Sori are in cups created by marginal flaps and scattered on the edges of the pinnae. The genus is named after August Dennstaedt (1776–1826), a German botanist.

Dennstaedtia punctilobula
Hay scented fern

TYPE AND SIZE Deciduous, 18–30 inches (45–75 cm) tall
HARDINESS Zones 3–8
DISTINCTIVE FEATURES Rhizomes are very long-creeping, going from state to state on the east coast of the United States. Lanceolate blades are bipinnate-pinnatifid, with pinnae carried in an almost ladderlike fashion and bearing glandular-tipped hairs. The glands give off a freshly mown grass fragrance, especially pronounced in dried fronds, earning the fern its common name.
ORIGIN AND HABITAT Here is a species that grows eagerly in acidic soil and is especially at home among the boulders of hillsides and roadsides in eastern Canada, the American Midwest, and particularly in New England and south.
GARDEN AND DESIGN USES Hay scented fern is quite tolerant of sunny exposures and turns russet in early autumn. Unless it is dutifully and regularly thinned, this species, while handsome, is not suited for a small garden but does serve as a scenic attraction in widespread, open, rock-strewn fields. It was Thoreau's favorite fern and one presumes he saw quite a bit of it. In cultivation, give it a site where it is welcome to roam.

DEPARIA

Until the late 1990s, most deparia were classified elsewhere, frequently as athyriums. *Deparia* is derived from the Greek *depas*, cup, and refers to the shape of the indusium in some species. The 40 or so species range from eastern Asia to Africa, with a few in North America and Europe. The deciduous blades are generally once-pinnate-pinnatifid. Plants are easily propagated by division and come readily from spores, which are in sori covered by linear or hooked indusia.

Deparia acrostichoides

Silvery glade fern, silvery spleenwort

TYPE AND SIZE Deciduous, 2.5–3.5 feet (75–105 cm) tall

HARDINESS Zones 3–8

DISTINCTIVE FEATURES Rhizome is short-creeping. Blades, which have silvery sori below and taper at both ends, are once-pinnate-pinnatifid clusters.

ORIGIN AND HABITAT This extremely cold tolerant species grows from Newfoundland south to Georgia and west to Minnesota. It can be found in moist glades, on damp slopes, and in shady woodlands. It is not suitable for dry sites.

GARDEN AND DESIGN USES Silvery glade fern is easily introduced to gardens, where its clumps of bright green foliage make a pleasant backdrop for darker greenery.

Deparia japonica
Black lady fern

TYPE AND SIZE Deciduous, dimorphic, 1–2 feet (30–60 cm) tall
HARDINESS Zones 6–9
DISTINCTIVE FEATURES The branching rhizome is short-creeping. Clumps of bipinnatifid sterile blades are oblong, and the taller fertile blades are narrower.
ORIGIN AND HABITAT Widespread in nature from the Himalayas, China, Korea, Japan, and Malaysia, this species grows in moist woodlands.
GARDEN AND DESIGN USES Dark blackish green fronds are a striking feature and should be used to visual advantage. Give it shade and a consistent supply of moisture. In the photo, it is in the center right, growing with *Epimedium epsteinii*, *Asarum pulchellum*, and *Dryopteris wallichiana*.

DICKSONIA

This stately genus offers some marvelous options for tree-fern enthusiasts gardening in Zones 9 and 10 as well as those dedicated to enjoying and overwintering them in Zone 8. Named for James Dickson (1738–1822), the genus has 22 species from montane tropical sites in South America and the South Pacific to temperate New Zealand and Australia. The type species is from the island of Saint Helena, which is probably better known for its association with Napoleon's final exile than for its botanical wonders.

With spreading canopies of bipinnate-pinnatifid to quadripinnate, leathery, 6- to 8-foot (1.8- to 2.4-m) fronds, dicksonias are recognized by having hairs but no scales on their skeletal support structure. Trunks are slow growing and slender, but are broadened significantly by the bundles of roots that extend from the trunk's apex to water and nutrients in the ground below.

Spores are carried in miniature cups along the frond's margins and are relatively short-lived. Logs from the trunks of *Dicksonia antarctica* are propagated much as one would root cuttings.

Dicksonia antarctica
Tasmanian tree fern

TYPE AND SIZE Evergreen, 15–20 feet (4.5–6 m) tall

HARDINESS Zones 8 (with an annual winter-insulating wrap) to 10

DISTINCTIVE FEATURES Trunks are from 10 to 20 feet (3–6 m) tall. Arching sprays of bipinnate to tripinnate, 6- to 12-foot (1.8- to 3.6-m) fronds are on very short stipes.

ORIGIN AND HABITAT This species is from Tasmania and mainland Australia. In nature, it enjoys humidity and soil moisture.

GARDEN AND DESIGN USES Of all the tree ferns, this is the one species most likely to succeed away from Zones 9 and 10. It is magnificent in wind-sheltered environments of cool coastal belts in Scotland, southern England, and California. In Zone 8, it needs an insulating winter life-support enclosure system. The type of insulation is unimportant so long as the fronds can breathe. Do not, however, use plastic or material that would magnify the sun's rays and scorch the fronds you're trying to protect.

Dicksonia fibrosa
Woolly tree fern

TYPE AND SIZE Evergreen, 18 feet (5.4 m) tall
HARDINESS Zones 9–10
DISTINCTIVE FEATURES The fibrous, rusty-colored trunk supports erect fountains of tripinnate to quadripinnate narrow fronds with short stipes. They are produced in abundance and reach a length of 8 or 9 feet (2.4–2.7 m). The species is readily recognized in the wild by the skirts of old fronds that droop and drape the trunk with blankets of cold-protective, dead fronds that even in their final life stage still serve a purpose. The pinnae have upturned margins that give the fronds a coarse texture.

ORIGIN AND HABITAT A New Zealand endemic, this is an interesting fern for moisture-rich soils where it can survive periods of frost. It is the most versatile of New Zealand's native ferns, accepting shade or somewhat exposed locales so long as the roots do not dry out.

GARDEN AND DESIGN USES In the landscape design, this is a stout and solid element with a height somewhat more home-garden proportionate than the *Cyathea* giants. Tidy gardeners need to adjust to the appearance of the dead skirts and resist the temptation to remove them; doing so might improve the fern's appearance, but it will hinder its cold resistance.

Dicksonia squarrosa

Rough tree fern, harsh tree fern

TYPE AND SIZE Evergreen, 12–20 feet (3.6–6 m) tall

HARDINESS Zones 9–10

DISTINCTIVE FEATURES This species is stoloniferous, sometimes forming multiple trunks. The narrow trunks are up to 20 feet (6 m) tall and embedded with the upright stalks of old stipe bases as well as buds that can produce multiple crowns. Bristles of outstretched dark russet hairs surround the old and the new growth and are an ornamental feature on the trunks, stipes, and emerging crosiers. Shiny, tripinnate fronds are rough or harsh to the touch, as the common name suggests.

ORIGIN AND HABITAT One of the most common New Zealand endemics, this species prefers shelter from wind and needs moist soil. The sturdy trunks are popularly used in construction. Look for sprouting walls in the landscape.

GARDEN AND DESIGN USES Watering requirements and wind protection need special vigilance on this species. Young plants are handsome in containers that will also slow their growth.

DIPLAZIUM
Twin-sorus fern

The genus name comes from the Greek *diplazios* or *diplazein*, to double, in reference to the two-valved indusium that splits open on both sides of a vein, a characteristic also reflected in the common name. More than 400 species grow worldwide essentially in damp tropical jungles and forests. They are deciduous or, on occasion, evergreen, with upright rhizomes and once-pinnate to tripinnate blades. The over-forty crowd may find some familiar-sounding names, but will recognize them as athyriums, from which they are now separated based on the *Diplazium* sorus or spore-bearing structure (plural sori), which is usually bivalved rather than hooked or crescent-shaped as in *Athyrium* of years past. All are easily propagated by division and/or spores.

Diplazium wichurae

SYNONYM *Athyrium wichurae*

TYPE AND SIZE Evergreen, 8 inches (20 cm) tall
HARDINESS Zones 7–8
DISTINCTIVE FEATURES Rhizome is creeping. Stipes are brownish purple at the base, green towards the top. The broadly lanceolate blade is a glossy forest green.
ORIGIN AND HABITAT This species grows in the rich, moist soil in forests of China, Japan, and Korea.
GARDEN AND DESIGN USES Evenly wet soil, such as that by a stream, suits this slow-spreading, handsome groundcover.

DOODIA ▸
Rasp fern

The doodias are a small genus of Southern Hemisphere ferns with rosettes of thick-textured, frequently colorful, stiff fronds. The plants have pinnae edged with marginal teeth that terminate in minute spines. A little stroking will find them rough to the touch. Blades are upright and once-pinnate with netted veins. Unfurling fronds are red, maturing to deep green.

This genus of about a dozen species is named for Samuel Doody (1656–1706), curator of the Chelsea Physic Garden in London, and England's first cryptogamic botanist.

These plants are marvelous options for tough, sunny and even dryish spots in the garden. For enhanced and prolonged color, grow them in slightly moist but well-drained sunny sites.

Doodia media
Common rasp fern

TYPE AND SIZE Evergreen, 12 inches (30 cm) tall

HARDINESS Zones 8–10

DISTINCTIVE FEATURES Most widely available and cold hardy of the doodias. There is also a crested variety.

ORIGIN AND HABITAT This species comes from New Zealand, Australia, Fiji, and New Guinea, where it grows in damp but well-drained sunny sites.

GARDEN AND DESIGN USES The raspy fronds will withstand partly sunny exposure and are drought tolerant once established. The new growth is a rich red and alarmingly late.

DRYOPTERIS
Wood fern, buckler fern

Dryopteris is a huge genus with more than 225 species and 77 hybrids at last count. It includes many elegant and functional plants from dwarfs for rock gardens to dramatic and majestic behemoths that are the sentinels of the landscape. The typical display features a shuttlecock of arching deciduous or evergreen fronds originating from erect or branching rhizomes. Some species are subevergreen (evergreen in mild but not cold winters). The emergence of signature scaly fiddleheads and stipes, with exceptional ornamental value, bring buoyancy to springtime.

The genus name is from the Greek *drys*, oak or forest, and *pteris*, fern, referring to its once common occurrence in oak woods. These are primarily ferns of temperate regions, with a concentration in the moist woodlands of eastern North America, Europe, Japan, and Asia. Most prefer rich, acid soils and once established are quite low maintenance, drought tolerant, and accepting of dry soils. When multiple crowns develop, dryopteris are easy to divide. They are also easily propagated from spores. Some species are apogamous, producing new plants without sexual fertilization.

European species, especially *D. affinis*, *D. dilatata*, and the circumboreal *D. filix-mas*, are noted for their tendency to produce sports (genetic variations). These were prized introductions reaching the zenith of their popularity as well as great monetary value in the British Victorian fern heyday. They still inspire a passionate following especially for the collector wanting something "different."

Dryopteris affinis
Golden-scaled male fern

TYPE AND SIZE Evergreen to subevergreen, apogamous, 3–4 feet (0.9–1.2 m) tall

HARDINESS Zones 4–8

DISTINCTIVE FEATURES The stout rhizome produces a thick crown, flush with sturdy sprays of lush foliage. The soft green new growth is handsomely dressed in translucent russet scales. The lanceolate blade is pinnate-pinnatifid to bipinnate. This species is similar in structure to *Dryopteris filix-mas* (male fern), but differs in having a small black dot at the base of each pinna where it joins the rachis. (It helps to have magnification and sometimes a stretch of the imagination to see this.) Classification of this species has been challenging for botanists (and consequently horticulturists) subjected over the years to many revisions. Current research, however, promises better understanding and by whatever name they are all garden-worthy subjects.

ORIGIN AND HABITAT This woodlander grows throughout Europe including the British Isles, western Russia, and Turkey, and extends its range into North Africa.

GARDEN AND DESIGN USES *Dryopteris affinis* is easily grown and handsome in almost any spacious garden situation—partial sun, shade, acidic, and even lime—it takes them all. Once established in the garden, it is drought tolerant. Although it can be deciduous in colder areas, it is fully evergreen in milder zones. The spring growth, covered in lustrous golden scales, is a truly elegant display, especially when backlit. With its inclination to clump, this species and its offspring can be readily propagated by division.

SELECTIONS

'Crispa Gracilis' ▶ Up to 8 inches (20 cm), excellent, tidy foreground specimen resembling a dwarf conifer.

'**Cristata**' ▲ Synonym 'Cristata the King'. From 2 to 4 feet (60–120 cm), crests at the apex and pinnae tips.
'**Revolvens**' ◀ Up to 2 feet (60 cm), with inrolled pinnae margins.

Dryopteris ×australis

Dixie wood fern

TYPE AND SIZE Semievergreen, 4–5 feet (1.2–1.5 m) tall

HARDINESS Zones (4)5–9

DISTINCTIVE FEATURES Rhizome is short-creeping and branches modestly. Fronds are a bold upright vase of pinnate-pinnatifid lanceolate blades, with the fertile upper portions reduced in size and bearing abortive spores.

ORIGIN AND HABITAT Like its parents, *D. celsa* and *D. ludoviciana*, this fern is native to dampish areas of the southeastern United States.

GARDEN AND DESIGN USES This is a popular, easy, and desirable garden plant that is especially useful as a vertical component in moist woodlands. The planting site should be protected from prevailing winds. The foliage reclines but remains green well into winter. Although southern in origin, Dixie wood fern is quite hardy in cold regions and adapts to locales with high summer temperatures as well.

Dryopteris bissetiana
Beaded wood fern

TYPE AND SIZE Evergreen, 2 feet (60 cm) tall
HARDINESS Zones 6–9
DISTINCTIVE FEATURES Rhizome is short-creeping, producing a rather horizontal spread of ornamental bi- to tripinnate fronds with a beaded appearance. New growth appears with a hint of silver and red.
ORIGIN AND HABITAT Like many of the truly ornamental dryopteris, this is from the woodlands of Korea, China, and Japan.
GARDEN AND DESIGN USES The beaded appearance is a unique addition to the charm of this rather slowly growing adaptable species. Use it in the formal foreground, where this feature is readily apparent and can be admired. Beaded wood fern is comfortable in warm as well as cool climates.

Dryopteris campyloptera
Mountain wood fern

TYPE AND SIZE Deciduous, 2 feet (60 cm) tall
HARDINESS Zones 4–7(8)
DISTINCTIVE FEATURES Rhizome is erect. The blades are thin-textured, triangular, and gracefully divided up to four times with significantly elongated lower pinnules.
ORIGIN AND HABITAT This fertile hybrid of *D. expansa* and *D. intermedia* is native and common in moist woods from New England to the southern Appalachian Mountains, where for the latter the range extends predominantly to higher elevations.
GARDEN AND DESIGN USES With a strong preference for woodlands and cold winters, mountain wood fern is easily established in partial sun or shade. Influenced by its *D. expansa* parent, it will wilt and perform poorly in areas with hot humid summers.

Dryopteris carthusiana
Spinulose wood fern, toothed wood fern

TYPE AND SIZE Deciduous, 1.5–2.5 feet (45–75 cm) tall
HARDINESS Zones 2–7(8)
DISTINCTIVE FEATURES The ascending rhizome produces clumps of airy triangular blades. The smooth foliage is bipinnate-pinnatifid and lacks glandular hairs. Early deciduous, it colors the Indian summer landscape with an autumnal butter-yellow warmth.
ORIGIN AND HABITAT This species is cosmopolitan and circumboreal in distribution with populations in the moist mountainous areas of northern North America, the Pyrenees, and the Himalayas. In the eastern United States, it is notably promiscuous and produces assorted hybrids that fascinate serious collectors and provide good entertainment and challenging excursions for the "weekend fern warrior."
GARDEN AND DESIGN USES *Dryopteris carthusiana* is an easy, adaptable fern although care should be taken to protect its somewhat brittle fronds from wind. Plant it in shade and loamy soil and forget it. Field characteristics are somewhat similar to *D. intermedia*, but the latter bears minute glandular hairs, is evergreen, and has more uniform-sized basal pinnae.

Dryopteris championii
Champion's wood fern

TYPE AND SIZE Evergreen, apogamous, 2–3 feet (60–90 cm) tall
HARDINESS Zones 5–9
DISTINCTIVE FEATURES Rhizome is erect and supports sparsely produced, airy, ovate, brilliant green bipinnate blades. The pinnae are widely separated, with the lowest pair thrusting sharply downward.
ORIGIN AND HABITAT In nature, this species grows in forests in China, Japan, and Korea.
GARDEN AND DESIGN USES With its lacquered upright winter-green foliage, this fern is truly a highly recommended champion. Look for fronds that persist and sparkle through snowy or dreary gray days of winter as well as the contrasting sultry days of summer. The showy young crosiers are temporarily fleeced with juvenile silver hairs and are among the very last to appear in the spring. Give it light shade and humus in a section of the garden that can be admired through frosted winter windows as well as summer garden strolls.

Dryopteris clintoniana
Clinton's wood fern

TYPE AND SIZE Deciduous to semievergreen, dimorphic, 2.5–3 feet (75–90 cm) tall

HARDINESS Zones 3–8

DISTINCTIVE FEATURES Rhizome is short-creeping. This hybrid of *D. cristata* and *D. goldiana* leans toward *D. cristata* in appearance, with broadly triangular lower pinnae but without the strongly horizontal pinnae habit. The deciduous fertile fronds are narrowly lanceolate, pinnate-pinnatifid, to 3 feet (90 cm), and the sterile fronds are evergreen and smaller.

ORIGIN AND HABITAT Clinton's wood fern is endemic to North America, sweeping across the wetlands of the northeastern United States and Canada. It is one of the most promiscuous of the so-inclined native North American dryopteris.

GARDEN AND DESIGN USES Here is a candidate for cold winter sites as well as warm summer habitats. The upright fronds are stiff and brittle, however, so protect them from wind as well as the peregrinations of local squirrels and your neighbors' dogs.

Dryopteris ×complexa

TYPE AND SIZE Evergreen, apogamous, 2–4 feet (60–120 cm) tall

HARDINESS Zones 4–8

DISTINCTIVE FEATURES This fertile hybrid has an ascending rhizome and massive upright fronds. The heavily scaled stipes are topped with lanceolate, pinnate-pinnatifid to bipinnate blades.

ORIGIN AND HABITAT This woodland fern from Europe and Asia is a cross of *D. affinis* and *D. filix-mas*.

GARDEN AND DESIGN USES The rusty-scaled new crosiers provide a dramatic springtime show, and the massive mature massif adds reliable year-round cold- and heat-tolerant substance to the garden design.

SELECTIONS

'Robust' ▼ Outstanding vigorous showpiece to 5 × 7 feet (1.5 × 2.1 m), drought tolerant, excellent for screening.

'Stableri' ▼ From 3 to 6 feet (0.9–1.8 m), strongly upright with narrow fronds.

'Stableri Crisped' ▲ Up to 3 feet (90 cm), narrow fronds with crisped and ruffled pinnae.

Dryopteris crassirhizoma
Thick-stemmed wood fern

TYPE AND SIZE Evergreen, 2–3 feet (60–90 cm) tall

HARDINESS Zones 4–8

DISTINCTIVE FEATURES Rhizome is stout and erect, and the crown is massive. The stipes are short, and the pinnate-pinnatifid to bipinnate blades are lanceolate. Pinnules have scalloped margins. The entire mass becomes winter procumbent with the arrival of early frosts.

ORIGIN AND HABITAT Widespread in northeastern Asia including Siberia and Japan, it colonizes in humus-rich forestlands.

GARDEN AND DESIGN USES With circles of stately, early-emerging, glowing foliage, this is an exceptional and highly recommended choice for light shade and average loamy soil in both warm and cold gardens.

Dryopteris crispifolia

TYPE AND SIZE Evergreen, 18–30 inches (45–75 cm) tall
HARDINESS Zones 6 (with protection) to 9
DISTINCTIVE FEATURES Rhizome is short-creeping. The beauty of this species is in the triangular blades, with their sparkling spun-glass green, tripinnate to quadripinnate crispy foliage.
ORIGIN AND HABITAT This species is endemic to the Azores and has demonstrated remarkable hardiness in the temperate Pacific Northwest through 10°F (–12°C) winters and rare (and unwelcome) 90°F (32°C) droughty summers.
GARDEN AND DESIGN USES With bright green fronds born on a procumbent plane, this is a cheerful accent for the mixed shady fern and floral bed in humus-rich soil. It is similar in dissection to *D. dilatata* 'Crispa Whiteside' but unlike the latter is not attractive to leafhoppers.

Dryopteris cristata

Crested wood fern

TYPE AND SIZE Deciduous to evergreen, 2 feet (60 cm) tall
HARDINESS Zones 3–8
DISTINCTIVE FEATURES Contrary to the name of this species, which was bestowed by Carl Linnaeus, this is not a crested fern. The erect fronds, which emerge from a short-creeping rhizome, are about one-third stipe and two-thirds pinnate-pinnatifid, bluish green, narrowly lanceolate blades. The slightly triangular pinnae, which are held parallel to the ground in an open Venetian blind fashion, give the species a unique profile.
ORIGIN AND HABITAT This species is native across temperate North America as well as Britain (where it is extremely rare), and central and northern Europe, including Russia extending eastward to Siberia. It grows naturally in wetlands, meadows, and moist forested areas.
GARDEN AND DESIGN USES Commonly cultivated in the eastern United States and comparable climates, this fern prefers consistently damp sites and rich soil, where with its unusual profile it offers visual variation. The plant does not do well in hot and humid summers, wilting even when well watered. Likewise, it shuns attempts at cultivation in coastal gardens in the western United States.

Dryopteris cycadina
Shaggy shield fern, shaggy wood fern

TYPE AND SIZE Evergreen, apogamous, 2–3 feet (60–90 cm) tall
HARDINESS Zones 5–8
DISTINCTIVE FEATURES Rhizome is short-creeping. The stipes are covered with dark scales that are especially prominent on young fronds. The once-pinnate blades are lanceolate.
ORIGIN AND HABITAT The shaggy wood fern grows in dark forests, often along streams, from 5000 to 8000 feet (1500–2400 m) in Japan, southeastern China, and Taiwan.
GARDEN AND DESIGN USES Growing as a symmetrical fountain of fronds, this two-toned duet of bright green and black is a natural beauty in shade and normal, humus-rich fern soil. The blackish new growth provides a welcome contrast as a backdrop for pastel spring flowers. For many years, it has been frequently and incorrectly marketed as *D. atrata*, a tender native of southern India.

Dryopteris dickinsii

TYPE AND SIZE Evergreen, apogamous, 1.5–2 feet (45–60 cm) tall

HARDINESS Zones 6–8

DISTINCTIVE FEATURES Rhizome is short and erect. The once-pinnate narrow blades are a refreshing light green and have shallowly scalloped pinnae. The lowest pinnae pair is shorter and inclined slightly downward.

ORIGIN AND HABITAT *Dryopteris dickinsii* grows in the moist forestlands of Japan, China, Taiwan, and India, where it is rare.

GARDEN AND DESIGN USES Here is an easy small to medium-sized fern that brightens woodlands.

SELECTIONS

'Crispa' ◄ Smaller with flowing wavy margins. Name means "curled."

Dryopteris dilatata
Broad wood fern, broad buckler fern

TYPE AND SIZE Deciduous to subevergreen, 2.5–4 feet (75–120 cm) tall

HARDINESS Zones 4–8

DISTINCTIVE FEATURES Rhizome is erect and produces an occasional offshoot. The frond blades are broadly triangular and tripinnate. The stipes are distinguished from many other dryopteris by their scales, which have dark centers framed by light brown borders.

ORIGIN AND HABITAT A variable species, the broad wood fern is quite cosmopolitan in acidic sites in Europe and parts of Asia.

GARDEN AND DESIGN USES This vigorous addition to the low-maintenance cool woodland will return faithfully in the ignored corner. It grows poorly in areas with extended hot humid summers. There are passels of varieties, many of which are far more handsome than the type. All, however, are susceptible to the disfiguration of leafhopper and/or thrip damage when these insects are present.

SELECTIONS

'Crispa Whiteside' ▼ Up to 2 feet (60 cm), broadly triangular crisped fronds.

'Jimmy Dyce' ▶ Bluish, 12–18 inches (30–45 cm), horizontal foliage.

'Lepidota Cristata'
Lacy, emerald green,
2 feet (60 cm), tips
crest.

'Recurved Form' ▶
Synonym 'Recur-
vata'. Up to 2 feet
(60 cm), pinnae roll
inward.

Dryopteris erythrosora
Autumn fern

TYPE AND SIZE Evergreen, apogamous, 2–3 feet (60–90 cm) tall

HARDINESS Zones (5)6–9

DISTINCTIVE FEATURES Rhizome is short-creeping and produces a bountiful spring crop of remarkable red-foliaged fronds. The shiny frond has bipinnate, triangular blades. In time, they fade to a glossy summer green, interrupted pleasantly on occasion by the arrival of an autumn-colored new frond. The sori, of the botanical *erythro* (red) and *sora* (sori), are covered by a bright red indusium.

ORIGIN AND HABITAT Autumn fern is common in the temperate forests of Japan, China, Korea, and the Philippines.

GARDEN AND DESIGN USES This species is admired for its universal adaptability and brilliance. Once established, the plant is drought tolerant. The evergreen winter fronds remain cheerful even when reaching above the snow.

SELECTIONS

'Brilliance' ◄ Emerging fronds strikingly orange red, hold color well into summer.

'Prolifica' Finely cut, smaller version of the type with propagable bulbils appearing sporadically along the rachis. The bulbils are more likely to be produced when the plant is stressed (inducing survival?). To propagate, simply prick off the bulbils and plant them in a moist enclosure, such as a pot capped with an inverted clear plastic cup.

'Radiance' A highly desirable, low-growing selection that emerges early in the season with saturated deep red foliage.

Dryopteris filix-mas
Male fern

TYPE AND SIZE Deciduous, 2–4 feet (60–120 cm) tall

HARDINESS Zones 4–8

DISTINCTIVE FEATURES Stout erect rhizomes support bouquets of fronds with dull green pinnate-pinnatifid lanceolate blades that taper at the base. This fertile hybrid is easily confused with *D. affinis*, with the most obvious difference being that *D. affinis* is evergreen to semievergreen and *D. filix-mas* is deciduous. A less obvious difference is that *D. affinis* has a small black dot on the pinnae underpinnings at the juncture with the rachis, whereas *D. filix-mas* does not.

ORIGIN AND HABITAT This hybrid of *D. caucasica* and *D. oreades* is a hugely common fern in Europe, where it grows at will in assorted habitats. Two distinct types are found in North America, with natives from western areas resembling the Europeans and the rare eastern plants choosing a limestone habitat instead. Its range extends to parts of Africa as well as most of Asia.

GARDEN AND DESIGN USES The common form can be planted and neglected and will faithfully reappear year after year. In *The Plantfinder's Guide to Garden Ferns*, Martin Rickard, who likes the fern, suggested using it in dark difficult sites "perhaps near the compost heap or site of the dust bin." It has a large number of varieties. As with other *Dryopteris* cultivars, these require precautions in sites that are subject to invasions from leafhoppers and thrips.

SELECTIONS

'Barnesii' Strongly vertical with very narrow foliage, 3–4 feet (0.9–1.2 m) tall.

'Grandiceps' ◄ Fronds with heavy terminal crests and small crests on pinnae tips.

Dryopteris filix-mas
(continued)

'Linearis Polydactyla' ▲ Fingerlike foliage with split ends throughout.

'Parsley' ▶ Up to 18 inches (45 cm), fronds variously and variably crinkled and crested. Cristata Group

Dryopteris formosana
Formosan wood fern

TYPE AND SIZE Evergreen (to deciduous in colder areas), apogamous, 18–24 inches (45–60 cm) tall
HARDINESS Zones 6–9
DISTINCTIVE FEATURES Rhizome is erect. The markedly pentagonal, lustrous, tripinnate blades are displayed on a horizontal plane (unusual for a *Dryopteris*). They are noted for the prominent elongated lower pinnules pointing downward from the lowest pinnae.
ORIGIN AND HABITAT This species is a native of forested areas in Japan and Taiwan.
GARDEN AND DESIGN USES Often overlooked, this drought-tolerant, easily cultivated fern offers a pleasant golden green sheen in average soil and exposure. The new growth usually emerges very late in the season.

Dryopteris goldiana
Goldie's wood fern

TYPE AND SIZE Deciduous, 3–4 feet (0.9–1.2 m) tall
HARDINESS Zones 3–8
DISTINCTIVE FEATURES The ascending rhizome is stout. The broadly ovate blades, in variable shades from bluish green to light pastel green, are bipinnate and abruptly contracted at the apex.
ORIGIN AND HABITAT Goldie's wood fern grows in moist woods throughout eastern Canada and the United States, although it is endangered in several states.
GARDEN AND DESIGN USES One of the tallest, broadest, and handsomest of east coast North American natives, this is suitable for cultivation in a wide range of temperatures. It hybridizes freely and is the parent of both *D. celsa* and *D. clintoniana*.

Dryopteris intermedia ▸

Fancy fern, evergreen wood fern

TYPE AND SIZE Evergreen, 1.5–3 feet (45–90 cm) tall

HARDINESS Zones 3–8

DISTINCTIVE FEATURES The erect rhizome sports a loose bundle of arching fronds of thin-textured bipinnate to trip-innate, ovate blades. The soft blue-green foliage is covered, especially on the undersides, with fine hairs tipped with round glands looking like Lilliputian hatpins.

ORIGIN AND HABITAT This species is abundant in acidic to neutral soils from moist hardwood forests and sandstone substrates to rocky slopes in northern and eastern North America as well as in the mountains of the southeastern United States.

GARDEN AND DESIGN USES Readily available, this is recommended as an easily grown all-purpose evergreen addition to cold temperate gardens, where it is cultivated in shady to somewhat sunny woodlands. This is one of the most promiscuous of the dryopteris, and the progeny carry the characteristic glandular hairs.

Dryopteris koidzumiana ◂

TYPE AND SIZE Evergreen or deciduous, 2 feet (60 cm) tall

HARDINESS Zones 7–10

DISTINCTIVE FEATURES A highly desirable relatively new introduction with stunning saturated brick red late (very) new growth. It displays well as an accent with pale green foliage.

ORIGIN AND HABITAT This species is from lowland forests of Japan.

GARDEN AND DESIGN USES Makes an outstanding specimen plant with its red new growth.

Dryopteris labordei 'Golden Mist'◂

TYPE AND SIZE Evergreen, 1–2 feet (30–60 cm) tall

HARDINESS Zones 5–8

DISTINCTIVE FEATURES A handsome cultivar with golden yellow-orange new fronds that warm the spring garden picture before maturing to a dark green. The blade is ovate, bipinnate.

ORIGIN AND HABITAT A Japanese selection of a species that grows in forests of Japan, China, and Korea.

GARDEN AND DESIGN USES The golden foliage attracts immediate attention wherever this fern is used in the garden.

Dryopteris lepidopoda ▸
Sunset fern

TYPE AND SIZE Evergreen, apogamous, 24–30 inches (60–75 cm) tall

HARDINESS Zones 6–9

DISTINCTIVE FEATURES Rhizome is erect. The bipinnate, glossy blades are broadly lanceolate. They emerge in richly decorative hues of salmon, orange, pink, and deep rose that subside into warm green tones. With the base of the blade squared and blunt (truncate), the frond looks like a glowing arrow.

ORIGIN AND HABITAT The sunset fern grows in mountainous areas from the Himalayas to China and Taiwan.

GARDEN AND DESIGN USES Here is a gem for average soil in the lightly shaded to early morning/late afternoon sunny ambiance of the woodland showcase. Additional colorful new fronds are produced throughout the summer, giving continued buoyancy to the display. The common name is perfect and accurately imaginative for this highly recommended beauty of an earthbound sunset.

Dryopteris ludoviciana
Southern wood fern

TYPE AND SIZE Semievergreen, 2–4 feet (60–120 cm) tall
HARDINESS Zones 6–9
DISTINCTIVE FEATURES Rhizome is short-creeping to erect. The mass of lanceolate dark green, shiny blades are pinnate-pinnatifid, tapering to the base with triangular lower pinnae. Reduced fertile pinnae are confined to the upper portions of the frond.
ORIGIN AND HABITAT Look for this fern in swamplands and borders of wet cypress woods, where it is frequently associated with limestone, in the southern swath of the United States.

GARDEN AND DESIGN USES Here is a selection for the difficult-to-manage muddy margins of ponds or bogs. It does not require lime or a swamp, although without irrigation it will not reach its potential in drier uplands. Give it a seriously hefty mulch in cool gardens. Unlike many eastern U.S. natives, southern wood fern does well in southern California and comparable areas. It is the parent, along with *D. celsa*, of *D.* ×*australis*, a better choice for gardens out of the southern wood fern's natural range.

Dryopteris marginalis
Marginal wood fern

TYPE AND SIZE Evergreen, 18–30 inches (45–75 cm) tall
HARDINESS Zones 2–8
DISTINCTIVE FEATURES The erect rhizome forms a single crown and a vase-shaped plant. The ovate, bipinnate blades are leathery and frequently bluish green. This species is easily identified by the sori that outline the edges of the pinnules, hence the common name.
ORIGIN AND HABITAT Look for this fern in rocky communities in woodlands and ravines and on slopes and walls in eastern North America. It is disjunct in Greenland.
GARDEN AND DESIGN USES This is a highly recommended species for growing in shaded, average soil with good drainage from the Rocky Mountains eastward, as well as Europe and Britain. For unexplained reasons it is reticent in the temperate areas of the west.

Dryopteris polylepis
Scaly wood fern

TYPE AND SIZE Evergreen, 2 feet (60 cm) tall
HARDINESS Zones 6–8
DISTINCTIVE FEATURES Rhizome is erect with fronds in arching sprays from short stipes. As the common name implies, the stipes are handsomely dressed in blackish brown scales that extend well up the frond. The narrow oblanceolate blades are pinnate-pinnatifid and a warm kelly green.
ORIGIN AND HABITAT This is a woodland species from Japan, China, and Korea.
GARDEN AND DESIGN USES Grow this fern for the excitement of the scaly new foliage. Give it light shade, where once established it is quite drought tolerant.

Dryopteris pseudofilix-mas
Mexican male fern

TYPE AND SIZE Semievergreen, 3–4 feet (0.9–1.2 m) tall

HARDINESS Zones 5–8

DISTINCTIVE FEATURES Rhizome forms a stout erect crown supporting a strongly upright dense shuttlecock of pinnate-pinnatifid fronds.

ORIGIN AND HABITAT This species grows at high elevations in Mexico, with populations extending into Guatemala.

GARDEN AND DESIGN USES This remarkably adaptable species is at home in an extreme assortment of climates from the very hot and humid to the rigors of winter extremes. With its dense stature, it can be used to define garden areas or to provide a dense background structure.

Dryopteris pycnopteroides

TYPE AND SIZE Evergreen, apogamous, 18–30 inches (45–75 cm) tall

HARDINESS Zones 6–9

DISTINCTIVE FEATURES Rhizome is erect with a swirl of pinnate-pinnatifid, narrowly lanceolate foliage. The pinnae have distinct, deeply scalloped margins. The lower pinnae are reduced but point neither forward nor downward.

ORIGIN AND HABITAT The true species is a native of forested areas in China.

GARDEN AND DESIGN USES With new growth that unfurls in a brilliant lime-green sheen, this fern is a welcome addition to somber areas of the shade garden. It is not fussy about soil or moisture. Water and mulch help it to adapt to areas with extended hot and humid summers.

Dryopteris remota

Scaly buckler fern

TYPE AND SIZE Semievergreen, apogamous, 2–3 feet (60–90 cm) tall
HARDINESS Zones 4–8
DISTINCTIVE FEATURES Rhizome is erect, with a bushy mop of bipinnate lanceolate blades.
ORIGIN AND HABITAT A hybrid of *D. affinis* and *D. expansa*, this rare plant is found in scattered subalpine areas in central Europe, Great Britain (including the shores of Loch Lomond), and Asia.
GARDEN AND DESIGN USES With its vigorous and refreshing early flush of bright green foliage, *D. remota* flourishes in bright filtered light and average soil and is drought tolerant. The dense clusters of fronds make it useful for low landscape screening or defining garden beds. Offspring may appear periodically but are not a problem. This fertile hybrid has the scaly crosiers of its *D. affinis* parent and the delicate texture of its *D. expansa* parent.

Dryopteris sieboldii

Siebold's wood fern

TYPE AND SIZE Evergreen, 18–30 inches (45–75 cm) tall
HARDINESS Zones 6–9
DISTINCTIVE FEATURES Rhizome is short-creeping. The unique open blades are leathery and ovate, looking like a *Pteris* on steroids, with two to five pairs of broad, linear bluish pinnae and a lengthy 6- to 12-inch (15- to 30-cm) terminal pinna. The new growth is significantly late.
ORIGIN AND HABITAT This species is found in the drier forests of Japan, China, and Taiwan.
GARDEN AND DESIGN USES *Dryopteris sieboldii* is not likely to be confused with any other ferns. Its bold fronds are a welcomed and admired feature in warm shade. In the Pacific Northwest and comparable climates, it can be frugal with frond production, but the annual output of large fronds is still positively stunning. By contrast, it is very partial to summer heat and is an outstanding performer in the American Southeast. Regardless of your temperatures, this is a unique conversation piece for the shaded garden.

Dryopteris sublacera

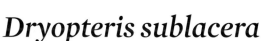

TYPE AND SIZE Evergreen, apogamous, 1–2 feet (30–60 cm) tall
HARDINESS Zones (5)6–8
DISTINCTIVE FEATURES The erect rhizome supports a rounded mound of thick-textured blades that are ovate-lanceolate and bipinnate.
ORIGIN AND HABITAT This species is native to high-elevation forests in China, Taiwan, and the Himalayas.
GARDEN AND DESIGN USES *Dryopteris sublacera* is a substantial, medium-sized selection for the moist to drier compost-enriched areas of the lightly shaded woodland. The glabrous upper surface is apple green, and the undersides are a complementary silvery green.

Dryopteris tokyoensis
Tokyo wood fern

TYPE AND SIZE Deciduous, 1.5–3 feet (45–90 cm) tall
HARDINESS Zones 5–8
DISTINCTIVE FEATURES Rhizome is erect, as is the structure of the fern. Stipes are significantly short, supporting lanceolate, narrow, and once-pinnate blades.
ORIGIN AND HABITAT Not surprisingly, this is a Japanese native, found as well in China and Korea, with populations in wet acidic soil.
GARDEN AND DESIGN USES Here is the ferny visual equivalent of a willowy tall grass, with slender arching fronds extending gracefully in a vertical reach. Tokyo wood fern is very useful for framing, especially at water's edge.

Dryopteris uniformis

TYPE AND SIZE Evergreen, 1–2 feet (30–60 cm) tall
HARDINESS Zones 5–8
DISTINCTIVE FEATURES Fronds emerge in early spring from an erect rhizome. Ovate-triangular blades are bipinnate, and fertile pinnae are produced exclusively on the narrowed upper third of the blade. They do not wither when the spores are dispersed.
ORIGIN AND HABITAT This species is a native of forested mountain areas of Japan, Korea, and China.
GARDEN AND DESIGN USES Easily grown in shaded, moist woodlands, this fern unfurls in concert and harmony with the early spring emergence of epimediums and brunneras under canopies of shrubby harbingers of the season. There is also a crested form.

Dryopteris wallichiana
Wallich's wood fern

TYPE AND SIZE Evergreen, apogamous, 2.5–5 feet (75–150 cm) tall
HARDINESS Zones 6–8
DISTINCTIVE FEATURES Warm, butter yellow, arching foliar pinnate-pinnatifid plumes erupt in mid to late spring from an erect rhizome. The short stipe is liberally coated with reddish black narrow scales that extend along the rachis.
ORIGIN AND HABITAT The range extends from the Mexican highlands to similar tropical mountaintop settings from South America to Hawaii. In addition, cold-hardy material is found in an amazing assortment of forested homelands, including Japan, China, and most of Asia.
GARDEN AND DESIGN USES As one of the most handsome of ferns available, Wallich's wood fern displays well against a contrasting rocky or stumpery background or wherever a bright highlight adds beauty and interest. Look for a most impressive display in the Hardy Fern Foundation collection at the Rhododendron Species Botanical Garden in Federal Way, Washington.

GYMNOCARPIUM

Oak fern

These dwarf delights are the elfin sprites of the fern world. Most are associated with moist, open, coniferous woodlands and the pleasures of leisurely strolls among wildflowers and ferns. They feature triangular to pentagonal, deciduous, moss green fronds waving on a horizontal plane from brittle upright stipes. Rhizomes are small and shallow growing. They travel in friable duff to create a loose woodland carpet of fronds. Sori without indusia are round to oval. Plants are readily increased by division and easily propagated from spores.

The genus name comes from the Greek *gymno*, naked, and *karpos*, fruit, referring to the absence of an indusium. Worldwide there are nine species, primarily from northern temperate areas. They are all wonderful garden-worthy ferns, charming even the undedicated.

Gymnocarpium dryopteris
Common oak fern

TYPE AND SIZE Deciduous, 9–12 inches (23–30 cm) tall
HARDINESS Zones 2 to (cool summer) 8
DISTINCTIVE FEATURES Rhizome is long-creeping. Blades are triangular to pentagonal and bipinnate-pinnatifid.
ORIGIN AND HABITAT Oak fern is found worldwide in shaded acidic soil, wet seeps, and varied woodlands in cool temperate zones.
GARDEN AND DESIGN USES This species is welcomed for its light airy effect and ease of maintenance in moist woodlands. It does not adjust to the hot summers of interior climates.
SELECTION
'Plumosum' ▼ With richly foliose fronds; even more ornamental than the type and naturalizes with equal ease. Name means "feathery."

Gymnocarpium disjunctum
Western oak fern

TYPE AND SIZE Deciduous, 9–12 inches (23–30 cm) tall
HARDINESS Zones 4 to (cool summer) 8
DISTINCTIVE FEATURES Rhizomes creep easily and widely. Blades are tripinnate-pinnatifid with extended lower pinnules.
ORIGIN AND HABITAT Look for this along the Pacific coast of North America from Alaska to Oregon and slightly inland to Montana and Wyoming. It can also be found in parts of Russia, Sakhalin, and Kamchatka.
GARDEN AND DESIGN USES This species gladly adapts to cultivation, creating a sylvan carpet so long as it is in shade, the soil is loose, and the moisture constant. Although it is a feathery attraction in cool temperate gardens, it does not perform well in hot summer areas. It is extremely similar to *G. dryopteris*, but it is larger and has tripinnate rather than bipinnate foliage.

Gymnocarpium oyamense

TYPE AND SIZE Deciduous, 8–12 inches (20–30 cm) tall

HARDINESS Zones 7–9

DISTINCTIVE FEATURES The slender rhizomes are long-creeping. Blades are long triangular and pinnate-pinnatifid with scalloped squared pinnule margins.

ORIGIN AND HABITAT This species is native to Japan, China, Taiwan, Nepal, the Philippines, and New Guinea.

GARDEN AND DESIGN USES An incredibly lovely species with a flowing soft texture, this is a soothing plant for cool temperate gardens. Give it shade, regular moisture, and humus-rich soil. Unfortunately, areas with hot summers are not suitable.

HOMALOSORUS

The single species assigned to genus *Homalosorus* is very close to *Diplazium*, which in turn is closely allied with *Athyrium*. The shape of the pinnae—entire in *Homalosorus*, pinnate or lobed in *Diplazium*—distinguishes the two genera for botanists, but has no visual impact in gardens where the delicate foliage is highly valued. The genus name comes from the Greek *homalos*, even or level, and *sorus*, a spore-producing structure, referring to the back-to-back (even) arrangement of the sori on the frond, a rare occurrence in ferns. Propagation is by division or spores.

Homalosorus pycnocarpos

Narrow-leafed glade fern, narrow-leafed spleenwort
SYNONYM *Diplazium pycnocarpon*

TYPE AND SIZE Deciduous, slightly dimorphic, 2.5–3.5 feet (75–105 cm) tall
HARDINESS Zones 4–8
DISTINCTIVE FEATURES Rhizome is short-creeping, producing clumps of upright, narrow, delicate foliage. Lanceolate, once-pinnate blades that taper at the base are statements of simplicity with outstretched, linear, 0.5-inch (13-mm) wide pinnae.
ORIGIN AND HABITAT The narrow-leafed glade fern sweeps across eastern North America from the Great Plains to the Atlantic Coast, with a few excursions into eastern Canada. In nature, it creeps about modestly in rich, neutral to slightly alkaline, moisture-retentive soil.
GARDEN AND DESIGN USES A favorite in east coast gardens, this slender upright fern offers ease of cultivation as well as a vertical diversion in woodlands. Keep it moist to prevent premature dieback in late summer.

MATTEUCCIA
Ostrich fern

With their huge vases of ostrich-featherlike fronds, these ferns are easily recognized and, in the proper situation, easily found. The world's three species are among the most cold tolerant ferns, growing in the severe and forbidding climates of Newfoundland and Alaska, with a comparable circumpolar distribution. However, their range extends to more accommodating regions including most of Europe, Japan, China, and Asia. Most plants do not perform well in areas with hot summers.

Characteristic long-creeping, branching stolons with wanderlust ramble about assertively just beneath the soil's surface and produce new plants at random intervals year after year. Strongly dimorphic (occurring in two distinct forms) fronds typify this rather primitive species. Sterile fronds unfurl with spectacular fistlike green balls in early spring. Fertile fronds, by contrast, are shorter, vertical, slender bottlebrush brooms that appear as greenery in late summer. Carrying beadlike sori, they overwinter as brownish black stems that to the uninitiated look rather like untidy dead stalks of perennials. The green spores mature in spring and are short-lived. However, with the fern's penchant for colonizing, there is little need for spores.

These robust ferns need ample room for their exuberant colonizing. Excess numbers of progeny can always be dug and given away and will be remembered as the "gifts that keep on giving."

The genus name honors Carlo Matteucci (1811–1868), an Italian physicist.

Matteuccia struthiopteris
Ostrich fern

TYPE AND SIZE Deciduous, 3–6 feet (0.9–1.8 m) tall or taller

HARDINESS Zones 2 to (cool summer) 8

DISTINCTIVE FEATURES Runners from the rhizomes spread ambitiously. The pinnate-pinnatifid sterile fronds, which are among the first ferns to flush in spring, are a brilliant green show of fiddleheads. In time, they reach 4, 5, or sometimes 6 feet (1.2–1.8 m) and are trimmed from base to apex with pinnae.

ORIGIN AND HABITAT Sweeps across the northern portions of North America from Newfoundland to Alaska and drops down into the coldest regions of the United States. Also populates similar cold habitats in Europe, Japan, China, and Asia.

GARDEN AND DESIGN USES Grows with enthusiasm in partial sun to full shade and damp to wet loamy soil. Readily introduced, the ostrich ferns cover woodlands and roadsides in much of the cool temperate areas of the world, but do not succeed in climates with extended hot summers. Plantings can become quite invasive.

SELECTIONS

'The King' A jumbo-trunked cultivar that can reach 8 feet (240 cm) is popular in the trade in the United States.

ONOCLEA

The name *Onoclea* is from the Greek *onos*, vessel, and *kleio*, to close or sheathe, in reference to the podlike pinnules enclosing the spores on the fertile fronds. Fossil records dating back 54 million years indicate that *Onoclea* was cosmopolitan in distribution until glaciation and the emergence of new mountain ranges restricted its range. Presently, there are only one to three species limited in native habitats to North America and Asia.

Onoclea sensibilis

Sensitive fern, bead fern

TYPE AND SIZE Deciduous, dimorphic, 2–3 feet (60–90 cm) tall

HARDINESS Zones 2–10

DISTINCTIVE FEATURES Rhizome is long-creeping and branching, producing fronds at frequent intervals. The triangular, papery-textured sterile blade is once-pinnate. The distinct, upright, unfernlike fertile fronds appear in late summer and carry spores in a series of green bead-like attachments that turn dark brown and woody as they mature. The encased spores are released in late winter or spring. *Onoclea sensibilis* is sometimes mistaken for *Woodwardia areolata*, which has minutely toothed rather than wavy margined pinnae, winged lower pinnae, and fertile fronds of narrow leafy tissue. When fertile fronds are present, the two are not likely be confused.

ORIGIN AND HABITAT This species is native to North America east of the Rockies and covers wide areas.

GARDEN AND DESIGN USES Sensitive fern is so ready to grow that eastern U.S. gardeners often reference it condescendingly. It should be kept watered but otherwise adjusts easily to all soil types and to all exposures from cold to warm climates. The fertile fronds ("seed heads") are popular and welcomed as long-lasting additions for dried flower arrangements. (Let the spores shed first, before spreading joy onto the table.) A handsome form with transient reddish new growth and persistent red stipes is a worthy addition to any garden's fernery.

ONYCHIUM

Onychium comprises eight to ten adaptable species found on the shaded forest floor or in partial sun from Africa, India, China, Japan, and the Philippines. The genus name is from the Greek *onychion*, claw. Characteristic lacy fronds, described by George Schenk as "more sky than substance," grow as clumps to 2 feet (60 cm).

Onychium japonicum
Carrot fern, Japanese claw fern

TYPE AND SIZE Evergreen to deciduous, 2 feet (60 cm) tall
HARDINESS Zones 7–9
DISTINCTIVE FEATURES Rhizome is short-creeping, producing a solid mass of vertical, airy, light green shiny fronds. The triangular foliage is finely divided (tripinnate or more). While usually deciduous, this fern can be evergreen in mild winters.
ORIGIN AND HABITAT Carrot fern can be found from India to high elevations in the Philippines in loamy soil with consistent moisture but good drainage.
GARDEN AND DESIGN USES This species is ideal and eye catching wherever the design begs for a feathery feature. Use it to lighten the surroundings in combination with heavy-textured ornamentals. Rhododendrons and kalmia come to mind, but other evergreens benefit from the contrast as well.

OSMUNDA
Royal fern

Osmundas are not ferny in the traditional sense of lacy green, frothy lightness that the word *fern* implies to so many. Look instead for sturdy, upright whorls of three or more fronds growing at the same level around a stem that serve as backdrops in perennial beds as well as in poorly drained garden lowlands.

These patriarchs of the fern world encompass 10 to 15 tall, moisture-loving, deciduous species that grow in acidic habitats and are extremely hardy and ornamental. Studies report that they, like so many ferns, are deer resistant. The fibrous black roots of osmundas are sometimes shredded for use in specialized potting mixes for orchids and assorted epiphytes. Stipes are frequently winged. The new growth is fleetingly downy, a down that is welcomed by hummingbirds for lining their nests. Autumn color is yellow.

Unlike ferns that bear their spores on the frond's undersides, osmundas carry their spores on modified fertile stalks and have no indusia. The green spores mature in days and have a shelf life of about three weeks. Refrigeration extends their viability somewhat, and freezing helps to improve their longevity. Although spores germinate readily, the offspring are frustratingly slow to develop into mature plants.

The genus name is credited to Carl Linnaeus, who reportedly named these ferns after the Nordic god Thor, who was in turn the Saxon god Osmund. A more romantic interpretation credits the name to Osmund, a Saxon waterman on Loch Tyne, who upon hearing of an impending invasion from the Danes hid his wife and daughter in great stands of *Osmunda* (apparently successfully).

Osmunda claytoniana
Interrupted fern

TYPE AND SIZE Deciduous, dimorphic, 2–3 feet (60–90 cm) tall

HARDINESS Zones 2–8

DISTINCTIVE FEATURES Rhizome is thick and upright. The unique fertile fronds have leafy tissue at the bottoms and tops, with blackish sporangia (spore-bearing structures) in the middle, hence the common name, interrupted fern. (It also leads some customers to wonder whether the middle is diseased.) The sterile upright fronds are pinnate-pinnatifid and do not have tufts of hairs at the base of the pinnae, thus distinguishing them from comparable fronds on *Osmundastrum cinnamomeum*.

ORIGIN AND HABITAT Unlike some of its brethren, this species does not grow naturally in marshes. It is native to parts of eastern Asia and the northeastern United States, where it is abundant in New England and the upper Midwest. Look for it on the grounds of Frank Lloyd Wright's Taliesin in Wisconsin.

GARDEN AND DESIGN USES This fern is easily grown in moist acidic soil in the partially sunny to the lightly shaded garden bed. With its exceptional cold tolerance, it is a welcome landscaping plant in cold-challenged areas.

Osmunda regalis
Royal fern, flowering fern

TYPE AND SIZE Deciduous, 2–6 feet (60–180 cm) tall or taller

HARDINESS Zones 2–10

DISTINCTIVE FEATURES Here is the royal fern and regal it is, with broadly ovate fronds occasionally up to 9 feet (2.7 m) on trunklike rhizomes. Bipinnate blades have opposite pinnae suggestive of locust tree foliage. The fertile portion replaces the leafy tissue at the tips of the spore-bearing fronds, hence the flowering of the alternate common name. New growth is briefly trimmed with silver down. Some botanists classify the robust European variety with its stalked pinnae as var. *regalis* and the slender American one with sessile (stalkless) pinnae as var. *spectabilis*.

ORIGIN AND HABITAT This fern is truly international, ranging from the extremes of snowy northern latitudes to semitropical habitats. In the wild, it is affiliated with swamps, marshes, and riparian sites, where it can form wide colonies.

GARDEN AND DESIGN USES Widely adaptable and cultivated, *O. regalis* and its varieties are noble and trouble-free for the beginning fern gardener as well as the specialist. The bold sprays of foliage are statuesque as backdrops or as focal points. Several ornamental cultivars can tolerate various exposures, including full sun in wet sites. All strongly prefer acidic soils. In upland gardens, supplemental water is a requirement.

SELECTIONS

'Cristata' ▲ Angular pinnae and crested frond tips.

'Purpurascens' ▶ Magnificent wine to purple new fronds, color persists on stipes.

OSMUNDASTRUM

Osmundastrum was recently separated from the genus *Osmunda*. There are currently two species: *Osmundastrum asiatica* and *O. cinnamomeum*. The vegetative foliage of the two can be confused, but the cinnamon fern's pinnae hairs at the pinnae–stipe connection provide the distinction between them.

Osmundastrum cinnamomeum
Cinnamon fern
SYNONYM *Osmunda cinnamomea*

TYPE AND SIZE Deciduous, dimorphic, 3–5 feet (0.9–1.5 m) tall
HARDINESS Zones 2–10
DISTINCTIVE FEATURES Rhizome is upright, trunklike, and occasionally branching. New growth is cloaked in decorative hairy silver froth, which in addition to being handsome is popular with hummingbirds for nest building. The common name aptly describes the highly ornamental plumes of erect fertile fronds that are covered with cinnamon-colored shaggy sporangial (spore-bearing) cases following the shedding of their green spores in late spring. The lanceolate vegetative fronds, which encircle the fertile fronds, have tall stipes and tufts of whitish to rusty hairs at the base of the pinnate-pinnatifid pinnae.
ORIGIN AND HABITAT This fern is common and locally abundant in wet acidic soils in eastern Canada and the United States down to the Gulf States, as well as the West Indies, Mexico, and South America.
GARDEN AND DESIGN USES The cinnamon fern is a very tolerant and willing garden subject. The fertile fronds wither early in the summer, and the sterile ones fade to a warm yellowish brown in autumn.

PELLAEA
Cliff brake

Pellaeas are mostly dusky blue charmers that enchant and taunt from cliff sides, mortared crevices, and other stressful, sunny habitats with dry and lean, gritty soil. A few non-xeric species have vivid green foliage. The rhizomes are short- to long-creeping. Stipes are thin. Evergreen, naked blades are once-pinnate to tripinnate. Sori, protected by reflexed inrolled marginal tissue, line the pinnule perimeters. The genus name comes from the Greek *pellos*, dusky, an apt description of foliage color.

There are 55 to 70 species, primarily of rocky dryland sites in the Western Hemisphere. In the American Southwest, they delight passing tourists in sites with spring bursts of desert wildflowers. While these sites are associated with fern-desiccating sunshine, often the fern's exposure is tempered by the shade of rocks that collect and funnel the minimal desert moisture to a relatively cool ferny root run. Adaptive foliage color is usually a sun-repellant blue. Ready-to-curl pinnae are an additional protective mechanism and will usually rehydrate with timely rain.

For most growers, the xerics are to be admired rather than cultivated. With attention to habitat requirements and lots of patience, they can be grown in temperate gardens, really. They want bright airy exposures, but not quite full sun, and turn spindly in too much shade. Tuck their long-ranging roots in moist but well-drained crevices in rocky sites and give them a gritty top dressing. They are good candidates for container culture, where they can be grown in customized soil and moved around when in need of attention.

Pellaea atropurpurea
Purple cliffbrake

TYPE AND SIZE Evergreen, 8–18 inches (20–45 cm) tall
HARDINESS Zones 4–9
DISTINCTIVE FEATURES Rhizome is short-creeping. The pinnate fronds are borne on dark purple-black stipes, a distinguishing feature.
ORIGIN AND HABITAT Purple cliffbrake is at home in limestone cliffs across central and midwestern North America, into Mexico and Central America.
GARDEN AND DESIGN USES Though none of the dryland pellaeas are easy to grow, even by inspired enthusiasts, this is one of the easiest of the group. It is suitable for a rock garden site with good drainage and a limestone substrate.

Pellaea rotundifolia
Button fern

TYPE AND SIZE Evergreen, 6–18 inches (15–45 cm) tall
HARDINESS Zones 8 (with lots of protection) and 9
DISTINCTIVE FEATURES Rhizome is creeping. The pinnate fronds arch and cascade in horizontal layers of shiny green round "buttons" of pinnae.
ORIGIN AND HABITAT This species is a New Zealand endemic and one of its most welcomed ferny exports. It is found in light scrub, dry forests, and occasionally in moist rainforest habitats.
GARDEN AND DESIGN USES A healthy and well-grown button fern is an extremely attractive addition to the indoor fern collection or patio displays in temperate Zone 9 gardens. It requires an acidic and well-drained grainy compost and, while it should not dry out, it is more likely to be lost by being overwatered. Give it good indirect light and occasional water.

PHEGOPTERIS
Beech fern

Depending on your age, the three *Phegopteris* species may be more familiar as members of the genus *Thelypteris*. The species are all temperate and, like their *Thelypteris* counterparts, ready to colonize—sometimes needing restraint—in woodlands of Zones 3 to 9. Rhizomes or runners creep just below the soil surface. With shade, moisture, and somewhat decent loam, beech ferns are undemanding and useful deciduous groundcovers. They are readily reproduced from spores carried in bundles of sori without indusia. Some species are apogamous, producing new plants without sexual fertilization. The genus name comes from the Greek *phegos*, beech, and *pteris*, fern, in reference to the plant's native origins under beech trees.

Phegopteris connectilis
Northern beech fern, narrow beech fern

TYPE AND SIZE Deciduous, apogamous, 8–15 inches (20–38 cm) tall

HARDINESS Zones 2–8

DISTINCTIVE FEATURES Rhizome is short- to long-creeping. Pinnate-pinnatifid to bipinnatifid blades are triangular with softly downy, thin-textured pinnae. Significantly, the lowest pair is smaller, points downward and forward, and is not fused to the rachis nor winged to the pinnae pair above. (Pinnae on *P. hexagonoptera* are connected by wings.)

ORIGIN AND HABITAT The northern beech fern is very common in cold temperate zones, heavily populating mountain slopes, woodlands, and mossy rocks across northern and eastern North America and Eurasia.

GARDEN AND DESIGN USES Grow this low creeper in shaded rock gardens, to define foregrounds of borders, unify stumperies, or wherever a mass of light greenery enhances the garden. New fronds emerge throughout the summer.

Phegopteris decursive-pinnata ▶

Japanese beech fern, winged beech fern

TYPE AND SIZE Deciduous, 1–2 feet (30–60 cm) tall
HARDINESS Zones 4–9
DISTINCTIVE FEATURES Rhizome is erect with short- to long-creeping root runners. Strongly upright blades tapering at both ends are pinnate-pinnatifid. The pinnae are broadly attached to the rachis and connected to each other by wings of foliar tissue (a defining feature of the species).
ORIGIN AND HABITAT This is the Asian member of the genus, with populations in Japan, China, Korea, Thailand, India, and the Himalayas growing in mountains, woods, walls, and rock crevices.
GARDEN AND DESIGN USES Easily established in light shade and moist woodlands, this fern is suitable for gardens from the warmth of northern California to the testing winters and summers of eastern North America, Britain, and Europe. With its upright soft foliar swords, it is a welcome groundcover, easily providing a green summer understory lasting well beyond the first frosts.

Phegopteris hexagonoptera ◀

Broad beech fern, southern beech fern

TYPE AND SIZE Deciduous, 12–24 inches (30–60 cm) tall
HARDINESS Zones 5–8
DISTINCTIVE FEATURES Rhizome is long-creeping, creating large stands of fern forests in moist woodlands. Broadly triangular blades are bipin-natifid. Lower pinnae are the widest, extending in triangular form from the base of the blade. All pinnae are broadly attached to the rachis and connected to each other by wings of foliage, an identifying feature. (*Phegopteris connectilis* has the lower pinnae pair distinctly unconnected to adjacent pinnae.)
ORIGIN AND HABITAT The broad beech fern is endemic to eastern North America, where it grows in acidic soils in northern states, but more abundantly in the southern coastal tier down to Florida.
GARDEN AND DESIGN USES This species is easily introduced to shaded and moisture-rich gardens, where it can be slightly aggressive but is easily controlled. Poor soil, a low-labor option, will restrain its spread somewhat. It is one of the last ferns to unfurl in the spring, but produces fronds throughout the summer.

POLYPODIUM
Polypody

Polypodiums, our many-footed friends, spread about, usually willingly, and their genus name, from the Greek *poly*, many, and *podion*, foot, refers to their creeping, branching rhizomes. There are approximately 150 species, with the greatest concentrations in the New World tropics. Many are epiphytes. Three temperate species—*P. cambricum*, *P. interjectum*, and *P. vulgare*—have produced numerous cultivars with crests and lacerations that are prized for their unique configurations and, in many cases, their rarity.

The roving rhizomes should be maintained on the soil's surface and not buried. The fronds, which are scattered along the rhizome, are pinnatifid to once-pinnate, with the exception of the cultivars, which can be ornamentally elaborate. Many species are leathery and evergreen, although some are winter green and summer dormant. Old fronds freely drop off the rhizome. Sori are round to oblong and without indusia.

Cultivation should be guided by the natural habitat of the species. Those from rock strata prefer a comparable gravelly garden position. Many take some time to become established and then proceed to colonize. Most of the temperate tree dwellers can adapt with ease in loose, leafy compost, where they can be left untended or, given their natural drooping tendencies, be displayed in hanging baskets. They are especially appropriate and ornamental as meandering plantings in stumperies. Other cold-hardy species prefer to wander among rocks or to creep along the tops of walls. Ornamental tropicals can be decorative in slightly humid home environs.

Spore propagation is annoyingly slow. Division is easy and practical.

Polypodium cambricum

Southern polypod
SYNONYM *Polypodium australe*

TYPE AND SIZE Winter green, summer dormant, 4–24 inches (10–60 cm) tall

HARDINESS Zones 6 (when heavily winter mulched) to 9

DISTINCTIVE FEATURES Rhizome is short- to long-creeping. Pinnate blades are ovate with the second from the bottom pair of pinnae the longest. The pinnae are frequently serrate. The species and all cultivars are summer dormant, producing a refreshing flush of fronds in late summer. They offer cheerful greenery throughout the winter and die back in spring.

ORIGIN AND HABITAT In its native southern European and British habitats, this species is found in mortared walls and occasionally in well-drained limestone soil.

GARDEN AND DESIGN USES Linnaeus gave the name *P. cambricum* to what is now known to be a fringed form of *P. australe*. However, because the original botanical epithet has precedence, the species and all of its cultivars are currently considered correctly classified as *P. cambricum*. By whatever name, they include some of the most desirable and interesting *Polypodium* variations. Although they tend to prefer limey sites, almost all acclimate in traditional moist, ferny loam. Arrange the unusual types in hanging baskets, where they can be displayed seasonally when they are dressed in foliage.

British collectors have selected and named a portfolio of varieties, some having been formerly classified under *P. vulgare*. Many are sterile and not reproductively available except by division. While many of these cultivars are featured in British and European gardens, only a few are in circulation in the United States.

SELECTIONS

Cristatum Group Segments and apex crested with the terminal crest narrower than the blade. 'Grandiceps Fox' ▲ is one member of this group.

Pulcherrimum Group ▲ Assorted cultivars with ruffled or shredded pinnae on simple stipes.

'Richard Kayse' ▲ Bipinnate with simple pinnae expanding to fringed pointed tips.
'Wilharris' ▼ Narrow leathery fronds with lacerated (torn) pinnae, 1 foot (30 cm).

Polypodium glycyrrhiza ▸
Licorice fern

TYPE AND SIZE Winter green, summer dormant, 1–2 feet (30–60 cm) tall

HARDINESS Zones 5–8

DISTINCTIVE FEATURES Rhizome is long-creeping. Blades are lanceolate and pin-natifid with pointed linear, smooth-margined pinnae. The rachis is unusual in having a smattering of hairs on the upper surface.

ORIGIN AND HABITAT This native of western North America is a common epiphyte on big leaf maples (*Acer macrophyllum*). The autumn combination of freshly emerging brilliant fronds with platters of butter yellow maple leaves is a magnificent sight.

GARDEN AND DESIGN USES Here is a species that will roam around in light soil without being invasive and is especially welcome as a winter cover where other plants are dormant. Conversely, it does leave a blank in the summer garden design.

SELECTIONS

'Grandiceps' ▸ Tasseled terminal tips.

'Longicaudatum' ▸ A long-creeper with an extended tonguelike apex.

'Malahatense' ▲ Sterile, slowly spreading, finely fringed form with pointed pinnae.

Polypodium interjectum
Intermediate polypody

TYPE AND SIZE Evergreen, 12–18 inches (30–45 cm) tall
HARDINESS Zones 5–8
DISTINCTIVE FEATURES Intermediate between its two parents, this polypodium is more robust than either. The branching rhizome is creeping. Unlike many polypodiums, this one has pinnatifid blades that tend to be somewhat oval. New fronds unfurl in mid and/or late summer, earlier than *P. cambricum* and later than *P. vulgare*.
ORIGIN AND HABITAT Look for this common hybrid of *P. cambricum* and *P. vulgare* on walls and among rocks in Britain and Europe. It prefers humid and high-rainfall sites with good drainage and slightly basic to neutral soil, rather than the acidic habitats of *P. vulgare*.
GARDEN AND DESIGN USES This fern is excellent in crevices and nooks, where the vivid greenery can relax the stark habitat and add lively winter color. Keep newly planted vertical sites moist (moss helps) until the roots reach the soil behind the structures.

Polypodium ×mantoniae 'Cornubiense'

TYPE AND SIZE Evergreen, 12–18 inches (30–45 cm) tall
HARDINESS Zones 5–8
DISTINCTIVE FEATURES A unique cultivar that randomly produces three types of fronds from standard to quadripinnate. Elegant and popular on both sides of the Atlantic, it spreads modestly in the garden.
ORIGIN AND HABITAT A selection of *P. ×mantoniae*, which in turn is a hybrid of *P. vulgare* and *P. interjectum* found in Europe and Britain. The cultivar, however, is readily available in the United States.
GARDEN AND DESIGN USES 'Cornubiense' serves well as a focal point in the winter garden. It tends to send up indecisive fronds midway between its parents.

Polypodium scouleri
Leathery polypody

TYPE AND SIZE Evergreen, 6–18 inches (15–45 cm) tall
HARDINESS Zones 8–9
DISTINCTIVE FEATURES Rhizome is wide-creeping. Like the frond, the stipes are thick and succulent. Glistening, deep forest green, pinnatifid blades are ovate with chubby lobed pinnae. *Polypodium scouleri* hybridizes with *P. glycyrrhiza*.
ORIGIN AND HABITAT This species is usually within a few hundred yards of the salty Pacific, from British Columbia and ocean fringes down to Baja California. In the Pacific Northwest, it settles in the dark crotches of the native spruce *Picea sitchensis*, dead or alive.
GARDEN AND DESIGN USES Neither salt spray nor decomposing spruce is needed to encourage the growth of this showy polypody in gardens with mild winters and cool summers. It prefers deep shade and acidic, friable soil. In spite of its leathery texture, this fern wilts in summer sun. An established colony will spread ever so slowly.

Polypodium vulgare
Common polypody

TYPE AND SIZE Evergreen, 6–15 inches (15–38 cm) tall
HARDINESS Zones 5–8
DISTINCTIVE FEATURES Rhizome is wide-creeping. Pinnatifid blades are lanceolate. New fronds appear in late spring to early summer, well before those of the related *P. interjectum* or *P. cambricum*.
ORIGIN AND HABITAT This polypody is common indeed, with populations throughout Britain, Europe, Africa, and Asia.
GARDEN AND DESIGN USES This fern colonizes at will on trees and as a groundcover on acidic soils in moist shade. It is the easiest of the British and European natives for cultivation.
SELECTIONS
'Bifidum' ▲ Forked pinnae.

POLYSTICHUM
Shield fern

Polystichums are magnificent in the landscape, ranging from temperamental alpines to stately and reliable ornamentals. Almost all the more than 200 species are evergreen. The fronds of these tidy plants are frequently shiny and usually have spiny pinnules with a prominent, genus-significant auricle (thumb) on the innermost portion of the pinnules. The new growth of many species is beautifully trimmed in silvery scales. Sori have a peltate (round and centrally attached tissue) indusium that opens like a wind-blown umbrella. The genus name, from the Greek *poly*, many, and *stichum*, stitches, refers to the pattern of the sori that stitch under the edges of the pinnae.

Most polystichums like light shade and moist but not wet soil. The challenging alpines require good air circulation and excellent drainage. Although they are accustomed to wintering under snow, they usually are not long-lived at lower elevations, so please do not try to collect them.

Several species produce bulbils and can be propagated by pinning these bulbils down in soft soil or by removing the buds and enclosing them in a mini-greenhouse atmosphere. An inverted clear plastic cup over a 4-inch (10-cm) pot placed in good light, but not direct sun, works nicely. Spore propagation tends to be erratic, but improves when spore is sown promptly from late-season rather than early-summer fronds. Some species are apogamous, producing new plants without sexual fertilization.

Old fronds do not have to be removed, but can be trimmed off to tidy the plant. It is easiest to attack the old foliage with one whack before new growth emerges in the spring.

Polystichum acrostichoides
Christmas fern

TYPE AND SIZE Evergreen, 1–2 feet (30–60 cm) tall

HARDINESS Zones 3–9

DISTINCTIVE FEATURES Rhizome is branched and creeps slowly, forming multiple crowns. The blades are lanceolate and pinnate. Fertile fronds are taller than the sterile ones, with the sporangia (spore-bearing structures) confined to constricted pinnae on the terminal third of the frond. These wither and turn brown when the spores are shed.

ORIGIN AND HABITAT The Christmas fern grows in Greenland and is abundant in eastern North America from Canada to the midwestern United States. It adapts to most soil types, likes shade, and is especially common in rocky deciduous woods.

GARDEN AND DESIGN USES This is the flagship fern of eastern North America. Popular, easily maintained, and not fussy about growing conditions, it is especially conspicuous and welcome in the bleak winter months. While it is a staple in the east, it has not been vigorous in west coast gardens, where for the best chance at success gardeners should start with a good-sized mature plant. Propagation by spores is easy. For immediate gratification, this is one of the few polystichums that can be readily increased by division.

Polystichum aculeatum ▼
Hard shield fern

TYPE AND SIZE Evergreen, 2–3 feet (60–90 cm) tall
HARDINESS Zones 4–8
DISTINCTIVE FEATURES Rhizome is erect, bearing vases of firm, dark green, arching fronds. The stipes are significantly short, but fat and heavily dressed in translucent russet scales. The lanceolate, bipinnate blade tapers strongly at the base.
ORIGIN AND HABITAT In nature, *P. aculeatum* prefers moist, lime-rich soils and can be found in shaded glens, ravines, and seeps in Britain, Europe, North Africa, and east to Turkey and the Caucasus.
GARDEN AND DESIGN USES This fern is a truly handsome addition to the garden, but it appreciates and will grow more vigorously in a basic compost. It can be confused with *P. setiferum*, but common names come to the rescue, as *P. setiferum* is the soft shield fern and can be distinguished by the soft feel of its fronds versus the hard of *P. aculeatum*.
SELECTIONS
'Cristatum' ◄ Twisting forks at the frond tips.

Polystichum andersonii
Anderson's holly fern

TYPE AND SIZE Evergreen, 2–4 feet (60–120 cm) tall
HARDINESS Zones 6–8
DISTINCTIVE FEATURES Rhizome is stout and erect and in time lifts the crown on a trunklike mass of stubble. The once-pinnate to pinnate-pinnatifid blade has deeply cleft pinnae. The blade is tipped with one or occasionally more bulbils that willingly reproduce when pinned down on moist humus in autumn.
ORIGIN AND HABITAT *Polystichum andersonii* is native to the temperate coastal regions of Washington, Oregon, California, and up through British Columbia to Alaska. It grows in leaf litter and shade.
GARDEN AND DESIGN USES This species is easily cultivated in west coast gardens, enjoying the naturally acidic soil. When in its exuberance it forms a small trunk, the whole should be lowered so that the crown is once again at the soil's surface. This is best done in early autumn.

Polystichum braunii
Braun's holly fern

TYPE AND SIZE Evergreen, 1.5–3 feet (45–90 cm) tall
HARDINESS Zones 3–8
DISTINCTIVE FEATURES Rhizome is erect. The shiny green fronds are dressed to the ground on short stipes. The lanceolate bipinnate blade is broadest in the middle and tapers symmetrically toward both ends, with the lower pinnae being less than 1 inch (2.5 cm) long.
ORIGIN AND HABITAT Braun's holly fern is rare and strictly northern in distribution, from the deciduous forests of North America to Europe and across Russia to Siberia and Japan, where it prefers shady habitats.
GARDEN AND DESIGN USES This boldly decorative species is strictly for compost- or humus-rich soil in cool or temperate lightly shaded gardens. It is not for warm or humid southern climes. While sometimes slow to establish, patience will be rewarded with a handsome and dependable evergreen.

Polystichum ×dycei

TYPE AND SIZE Evergreen, 2.5–3.5 feet (75–105 cm) tall
HARDINESS Zones (6)7–8
DISTINCTIVE FEATURES Rhizome is stout, with an imposingly robust crown. Stipes are very short. The bipinnate-pinnatifid blade is broadest approaching the top third. Like *P. braunii*, the blade tapers at the base and is in full foliar dress to the ground. One to three propagable bulbils are on the fronds' undersides close to the apex.
ORIGIN AND HABITAT A cross between *P. proliferum* and *P. braunii*, this hybrid is one of several that can call a laboratory home. This fern was created by the late Anne Sleep of Leeds University in Britain. Many of her hybrids involved a parent with a bulbil that persists in the progeny, thus encouraging further propagation.
GARDEN AND DESIGN USES This vigorous, sterile hybrid grows rapidly in light compost and is one of the very best evergreens for dappled shade. It is an easy showpiece with a giant horizontal wheel of foliage and consistently brings admiring compliments from visitors.

Polystichum makinoi
Makino's holly fern

TYPE AND SIZE Evergreen, 18–30 inches (45–75 cm) tall
HARDINESS Zones 5–9
DISTINCTIVE FEATURES Rhizome is erect. Forest green, bipinnate, luminescent blades are lanceolate.
ORIGIN AND HABITAT This fern grows in humus-rich duff in the forests of Japan, China, Taiwan, and the Himalayas.
GARDEN AND DESIGN USES Here is an outstanding beauty adapted to temperate gardens of all climatic persuasions. Give it compost, light shade, and the subtle company of matte foliage for a magnificent garden panorama. Makino's holly fern also serves well in flower arrangements and is likely to outlast the flowers.

Polystichum munitum
Western sword fern

TYPE AND SIZE Evergreen, 3–5 feet (0.9–1.5 m) tall
HARDINESS Zones 6–9
DISTINCTIVE FEATURES Rhizome is erect and supports bushels of
swordlike lush foliage, sometimes up to 50 fronds per clump. The
linear-lanceolate blade is once-pinnate with pinnae prominently auri-
cled (having a thumb).
ORIGIN AND HABITAT *Polystichum munitum* is the ubiquitous understory fern in the soft decomposing-needle compost of coniferous forests from Alaska and British Columbia to California, with an occasional
disjunct station in Mexico and South Dakota.
GARDEN AND DESIGN USES Were this species rare, there would be a
tremendous demand (and price) for it. Adaptable, weather-resistant,
and a multipurpose ornamental, the sword fern has "good bones" and
settles with ease in maritime-moderated temperate climates. It is highly
recommended, as are most natives, as one of the best for beginning
fern gardeners in the Pacific Northwest. Although unfazed when frequently snowbound in its native haunts, western sword fern suffers and
declines in the typical summer heat and humidity of the eastern and
southern United States.

Polystichum neolobatum
Asian saber fern, long-eared holly fern

TYPE AND SIZE Evergreen, apogamous, 18–30 inches (45–75 cm) tall
HARDINESS Zones 5–8
DISTINCTIVE FEATURES Rhizome is erect. The stipes are barely visible under the lush coating of papery, reddish brown prominent scales.
The polished blade, bipinnate at the base, is lanceolate with severely
spiny pinnae. This species is quite variable with two somewhat different
forms in circulation. The type described here has been widely distributed and is representative of the material included in Japanese floras.
Himalayan natives are more succulent in appearance, with a deeper,
green gloss and are not as sharp to the touch.
ORIGIN AND HABITAT *Polystichum neolobatum* grows in and around forests from the Himalayas to Myanmar, China, Taiwan, and Japan.
GARDEN AND DESIGN USES Here is a true aristocrat that is a well-
behaved, reliable, and beautiful specimen throughout the year. Fronds
remain upright in snowstorms, and new growth emerges in early spring.
While very tolerant of hot and humid sites, the sun will scorch the foliage, so plant it in the shade.

Polystichum polyblepharum
Tassel fern, bristle fern

TYPE AND SIZE Evergreen, 1.5–3 feet (45–90 cm) tall
HARDINESS Zones 6–9
DISTINCTIVE FEATURES Rhizome is erect. In time, it can form a trunk that is 4–5 inches (10–13 cm) in both height and diameter, at which point it should be replanted to keep the crown at soil level. Stipes emerge sheathed in silver scales. The bipinnate, ovate-lanceolate blades are exceptionally lustrous.
ORIGIN AND HABITAT The tassel fern is another of the fine imports from China, Korea, and Japan, where it is very common.
GARDEN AND DESIGN USES This striking fern arrived in the gardens of North American hobbyists in the 1960s as a by-product of the florist trade. The Miller Botanical Garden's Great Plant Picks Program chose this beauty above all others as the first fern to be included in its recommendations. Plant it in rich soil and shade with a consistently and reliably moist root zone. So long as it is not allowed to dry out, tassel fern acclimates in areas with hot summers and as a bonus is useful in flower arrangements.

Polystichum retrosopaleaceum

TYPE AND SIZE Evergreen, 2–3 feet (60–90 cm) tall
HARDINESS Zones 5–8
DISTINCTIVE FEATURES Rhizome is erect, supporting rosettes of lax arching lanceolate bipinnate blades with downward-pointing basal pinnae.
ORIGIN AND HABITAT Large populations grow in rich soil throughout forests in Korea and especially Japan.
GARDEN AND DESIGN USES An easily cultivated hardy fern, this species awakens in early spring. Plant it where the refreshing and welcome "spring is finally here" early crosiers can be admired. It can be differentiated from the extremely similar *P. ovatopaleaceum* by the scales that aim downward rather than upward, as in the latter.

Polystichum richardii
Richard's holly fern, black shield fern

TYPE AND SIZE Evergreen, 1–2 feet (30–60 cm) tall
HARDINESS Zones 8 (with protection) and 9
DISTINCTIVE FEATURES Rhizome is erect. The name is confused in the trade. By whatever name, the blades are ovate-lanceolate, sumptuous deep forest green, and bi-pinnate. In 2003, taxonomists divided this variable species into four taxa: *P. neozelandicum* subsp. *neozelandicum*, *P. neozelandicum* subsp. *zerophyllum*, *P. oculatum*, and *P. wawranum*. Notice that the name *P. richardii* is nowhere in sight. For field characteristics, differences are based on scale size and shape, distance between pinnae, the size of the dark center in the indusia, and somewhat on geographical distribution. Naturally, these all grade into each other. Take your choice.
ORIGIN AND HABITAT Endemic to New Zealand, these ferns are found in varied habitats.
GARDEN AND DESIGN USES In general, the erstwhile *P. richardii* with its magnificently dark and shiny, blackish green foliage is readily recognizable. In cultivation, it grows in assorted soil types, but unfortunately, it is only border-line hardy in Zone 8. For best results, it needs protection or a life in the comfort of Zones 9–11, or it can provide indoor cheer anywhere.

Polystichum rigens

TYPE AND SIZE Evergreen, apogamous, 18 inches (45 cm) tall
HARDINESS Zones 6–8
DISTINCTIVE FEATURES The rhizome is erect. Radiant, narrowly triangular blades are bipinnate.
ORIGIN AND HABITAT *Polystichum rigens* is a rare species from the montane forests of China and Japan.
GARDEN DESIGN AND USES This increasingly available attractive import is slow growing and prefers a site enriched with compost in full shade. When young it gives off a slight "eau de skunk," which is not distracting in the garden but can attract circumspect comments when gathered in the greenhouse. Use it as a tidy edging with year-round interest.

Polystichum setiferum
Soft shield fern

TYPE AND SIZE Evergreen, 2–3 feet (60–90 cm) tall
HARDINESS Zones 6–8
DISTINCTIVE FEATURES Rhizome is erect, supporting wide fans of soft, willowy fronds. Stipes are coated with glittering silver scales on emerging fiddleheads. The bipinnate, lanceolate blade is broadest in the middle.
ORIGIN AND HABITAT Soft shield fern is common in Britain and Europe, where it grows in hedgerows and in deciduous woodlands. It is best in neutral soil.
GARDEN AND DESIGN USES Plant this species and its cultivars in a moist, but not wet, lightly shaded environment and give it room to let its lax fronds billow. It and the plumose types are particularly attractive when planted en masse on slopes.
SELECTIONS
Bevis Group ◀ Includes the most cherished treasure(s) among the *P. setiferum* cultivars. Finely divided evergreen fronds mature at 2–3 feet (60–90 cm). Sterile, but fortunately this group is currently being produced by tissue culture. In addition, the occasional and rarely produced spore yields prize results.
'Congestum' Up to 10 inches (25 cm), dwarf with dense clusters of foliage.
'Congestum Cristatum' As 'Congestum' with mildly crested frond tips.
'Cristatopinnulum' Up to 2 feet (60 cm), open sprays of bright green fringe.
Cristatum Group With varying degrees of forking and cresting at the pinnae and/or frond tips.
Divisilobum Group ▶ Divisilobum refers to the divided lobes. The group includes the most readily available and signature cultivars from varied *P. setiferum* offerings. Plants are finely cut and often tripinnate, with a horizontal tendency for the graceful 2-foot (60-cm) fronds. Bulbils are produced along the rachis and root willingly. This is the British fern known inaccurately in the U.S. trade as the "Alaska fern."
'Herrenhausen' From 2 to 3 feet (60–90 cm), lacy dark green divisilobum plumes.
'Lineare' Up to 2 feet (60 cm), with bipinnate skeletal airy fronds.

'Percristatum' Crested throughout.

Plumosodivisilobum Group ◄ Name refers to feathery, divided lobes. The group includes some of the most beautiful and feathery fern cultivars ever discovered. Fronds are open-spaced layers of gossamer green and up to quadripinnate (an ultimate in division).

Plumosomultilobum Group ▼ Name refers to feathery, multiple lobes. An especially magnificent quadripinnate collection of beauties that make impressive and graceful understory evergreens. (These are often offered as 'Plumosodensum' or 'Plumosomultilobum'.) Pinnae and pinnules overlap, producing a dense froth of pale green fronds that often extend in a sweeping horizontal whorl of three or more growing at the same level around a stem. These are appreciated and enjoyed whenever and wherever available and reproduce easily when bulbils are produced.

'Rotundatum Cristatum' Up to 3 feet (90 cm), bipinnate, rounded pinnules, large terminal forks, produces copious quantities of easy to grow bulbils.

Polystichum tsus-simense

Tsus-sima holly fern, Korean rock fern

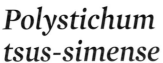

TYPE AND SIZE Evergreen, apogamous, 12–18 inches (30–45 cm) tall

HARDINESS Zones 6–9

DISTINCTIVE FEATURES Rhizome is erect. Blades are lanceolate, bipinnate, and blackish green with darker veins.

ORIGIN AND HABITAT This fern is found in forests and rocky sites in China, Thailand, Cambodia, Laos, Vietnam, Japan, and Korea.

GARDEN AND DESIGN USES *Polystichum tsus-simense* arrived in North America via the florist trade, where it is a popular finishing touch for boutonnieres. Garden hardiness and worthiness came as an unexpected bonus. It is a tidy low-growing trimming for shady perennial beds, as well as a very suitable low-maintenance choice for indoor culture.

Polystichum vestitum

Prickly shield fern

TYPE AND SIZE Evergreen, 1–3 feet (30–90 cm) tall

HARDINESS Zones (6)7–8

DISTINCTIVE FEATURES Rhizome is erect. Polystichums are noted for their heavy sheaves of stipe scales, and this species is among the most handsomely decorated of all. The blades are lanceolate and bipinnate.

ORIGIN AND HABITAT This native of fern-rich New Zealand is common throughout the country and especially plentiful on the hillsides of the South Island. Fern-enlightened tourists can delight in its presence near the popular New Zealand destinations of Queenstown and Milford Sound.

GARDEN AND DESIGN USES The species has no particular soil preference and is a graceful bouquet in lightly shaded woodlands. It is somewhat more sun tolerant than other polystichums.

Polystichum xiphophyllum

TYPE AND SIZE Evergreen, apogamous, 18 inches (45 cm) tall

HARDINESS Zones (6)7–8

DISTINCTIVE FEATURES The rhizome is erect. The lanceolate once-pinnate blades have a silvery green patina and the detached auricle (thumb) is prominent, giving the pinnae an upward-running trail adjacent to the rachis.

ORIGIN AND HABITAT This is a rare species from China, Taiwan, and India.

GARDEN AND DESIGN USES *Polystichum xiphophyllum* is a lovely, increasingly popular, low-growing ornamental with a simple horizontal presentation. Use it as a unifying groundcover under shade-loving floral uprights.

PTERIS

Brake fern

The approximately 300 *Pteris* species are cosmopolitan in distribution but mostly tropical. Many serve as decorations in homes. The genus name is derived from the Greek *pteron*, fern or wing, a definition that captures the silhouette of the pinnae. The common name refers to the resemblance of the proportionately long stipes to the similarly long legs of the bracken fern (*Pteridium*).

The rhizomes are generally erect but occasionally short-creeping. Evergreen to deciduous blades have very few sets of widely separated long and narrow winglike pinnae. The sori surround the outer pinnae edges and are enclosed in recurved marginal tissue. Many brake ferns are dimorphic (occurring in two distinct forms), with slender upright fertile fronds. All the species described here are apogamous, producing new plants without sexual fertilization.

Growers looking for variegation will find many options among the cultivars. All are good choices for indoors. As with most ferns, they should have loose potting soil and good drainage and not be overwatered.

Pteris cretica
Ribbon fern, Cretan brake

TYPE AND SIZE Evergreen to deciduous, dimorphic, apogamous, 1–2 feet (30–60 cm) tall

HARDINESS Zones 8–10

DISTINCTIVE FEATURES Rhizome is short-creeping. Once-pinnate, ovate blades have two to four pairs of linear pinnae. The sterile fronds hover horizontally, whereas the fertile fronds are narrow and upright.

ORIGIN AND HABITAT This species grows worldwide from tropical and subtropical areas to an occasional montane habitat. Ribbon fern has naturalized so extensively that the true native range is uncertain. It is found among boulders and exposed rocky meadows in partial sun to shade.

GARDEN AND DESIGN USES Truly a willing plant, ribbon fern needs only good indirect light, well-draining soil, and occasional, but not excessive, watering.

SELECTIONS
'Albo-lineata' Bicolored white and green, narrow fronds.

Pteris vittata
Ladder brake

TYPE AND SIZE Evergreen to deciduous, apogamous, 1–3 feet (30–90 cm) tall

HARDINESS Zones (8)9–10

DISTINCTIVE FEATURES Rhizome is compact. Once-pinnate blades are lanceolate with ladderlike horizontal pinnae.

ORIGIN AND HABITAT The ladder brake is native to Europe, Asia, and South America and has naturalized over a wide area of the southern United States. It prefers limestone sites from walls to forested areas with basic soils.

GARDEN AND DESIGN USES This species is easily introduced to warm gardens. However, since it was discovered that it absorbs arsenic from soil and water, ladder brake has received some well-deserved press and wide distribution for recovery projects, where it is efficiently removing toxins.

PYRROSIA

Felt fern

Pyrrosias are unfernlike in appearance, and their common name describes the coating of hairy silver stars that decorates unfurling fronds. These mature to a soft, feltlike, rusty blanket that persists on the underside of the frond and protects the indusia-free developing spores. The genus name is derived from the Greek *pyrros*, flame or fire, in reference to the rusty hairs.

Rhizomes are short- to long-creeping, with those of many species slender and wiry, whereas others are thick and stubby. Sentinels of round, elliptical, or vertical tongues of simple, undivided blades may be densely packed or widely separated as the rhizome creeps forward. Sori without indusia are often camouflaged under the protection of the starry canopy. Spores are yellow. Most do not mature until late winter, when they drop yellowish gold dust that could easily be mistaken for some mysterious alien pollen. Propagation is easily accomplished by division and not so promptly by spores.

With their distinctive, nontraditional structure, these are plants to be featured in special sites. They are impressively drought tolerant even in their preferred coarse, good-draining mix. There are 50 to more than 70 species spreading across a broad spectrum of homelands. When used for garden enrichment, these distinguished ferns are guaranteed to please the grower and surprise the uninitiated with their unusual silhouettes. There is a wide assortment of seriously unique cultivars.

Pyrrosia lingua ▶

Tongue fern, felt fern

TYPE AND SIZE Evergreen, 8–15 inches (20–38 cm) tall
HARDINESS Zones 7b (in warm summer areas) and 8 (with protection) to 10
DISTINCTIVE FEATURES The branching wiry rhizome is long-creeping and supports a vigorous display of leathery foliage. The blades are simple and upright with a tapered base.
ORIGIN AND HABITAT This species grows among dryish rocks and on tree trunks in China, Korea, Taiwan, and Japan.
GARDEN AND DESIGN USES This species and its cultivars are magnificent and popular display features in conservatories or Zones 8 (with protection) to 10, where they can roam at will. Elsewhere they are showy container plants. The species produces many curious and unique varieties, especially from Japan. Look for them in the connoisseurs' trade.
SELECTIONS
'Corymbifera' Up to 12 inches (30 cm), broad fans of mild crests on frond tips.
'Eboshi' Up to 8 inches (20 cm), twisted fronds curl in clumps.
'Kei Kan' Up to 8 inches (20 cm), randomly fringed edges.
'Ogon Nishiki' Up to 12 inches (30 cm), irregularly marked with yellow variegation.
'Shishi' From 6 to 8 inches (15–30 cm), compact and finely crested.

Pyrrosia polydactyla ▾

TYPE AND SIZE Evergreen, 8–12 inches (20–30 cm) tall

HARDINESS Zone 8 (with protection) to 10

DISTINCTIVE FEATURES Rhizome is short-creeping. Upright stipes support semi-circles of palmate, three- to five-lobed, interesting horizontal blades.

ORIGIN AND HABITAT This delightful departure from the traditional image of ferniness is an endemic species of Taiwan, where it grows in rocky habitats with lean soil.

GARDEN AND DESIGN USES Although truly drought tolerant, this conversation piece will curl up when severely underwatered, but it returns to life undamaged when rehydrated and so should be sited accordingly or used in a container.

Pyrrosia sheareri

TYPE AND SIZE Evergreen, 1–2 feet (30–60 cm) tall
HARDINESS Zones 7–10
DISTINCTIVE FEATURES Rhizome is short-creeping. Simple blades unfurl in downy silver fleece and at maturity are leathery and frequently heart shaped at the base.
ORIGIN AND HABITAT In typical *Pyrrosia* fashion, this species grows on rocks and trees in Taiwan, China, and Vietnam.
GARDEN AND DESIGN USES Defying its rather tropical aura, *P. sheareri* will thrive through temperatures below 10°F (–12°C). With its unconventional appearance, it amazes visitors. "That's a fern?" Plant it as a focal point in the garden or container with porous, humus-rich soil, an occasional nip from the hose, and an annual trimming of spent foliage to keep it in good health.

RUMOHRA

Rumohra was named in honor of Karl von Rumohr (1785–1843), an artist from Dresden, Germany. The handful of species are Southern Hemisphere natives.

Rumohra adiantiformis
Leatherleaf fern

TYPE AND SIZE Evergreen, to 3 feet (90 cm) tall

HARDINESS Zones 8–10, although plants may lose foliage in cold winter areas

DISTINCTIVE FEATURES Creeping rhizomes support bi- to tripinnate triangular blades. The fronds of leatherleaf fern are those familiar glossy adornments that give the finishing touch to flower arrangements (and long outlive the flowers).

ORIGIN AND HABITAT Native to Chile, this species grows in sunny sites at high elevations.

GARDEN AND DESIGN USES Grow it in filtered shade and average compost. In cooler climates, it is a decorative houseplant needing good light to keep from becoming leggy and space to stretch its lustrous foliage. Economically, leather leaf fern fronds are of great commercial significance as a cut foliage crop.

THELYPTERIS
Maiden fern

The wide-ranging populations of *Thelypteris* are attractively functional in supporting miles of roadside banks in the eastern United States and elsewhere. They are uniformly deciduous with hairy foliage and grow from creeping rhizomes. Sori are often naked or briefly covered with a kidney-shaped indusium. The genus name comes from the Greek *thelys*, female, and *pteris*, fern. Depending on interpretations of current taxonomy, there are as few as 30 to as many as 1000 species worldwide. Most are tropical.

Thelypteris kunthii
Southern maiden fern

TYPE AND SIZE Deciduous, 2–4 feet (60–120 cm) tall
HARDINESS Zones 8–10
DISTINCTIVE FEATURES With a rhizome that is short- to long-creeping, this species produces bushes of pinnate-pinnatifid blades that are lanceolate to narrowly triangular.
ORIGIN AND HABITAT This is native to the southeastern United States, where it grows in roadside ditches and riparian habitats.
GARDEN AND DESIGN USES Popular for its low maintenance and heat tolerance, this easily introduced species is a common choice in difficult areas of the American South. Use it with care in moisture-rich sites where a quick cover is welcome.

Thelypteris noveboracensis ▸

Tapering fern, New York fern
SYNONYM *Parathelypteris noveboracensis*

TYPE AND SIZE Deciduous, 1–2 feet (30–60 cm) tall
HARDINESS Zones 4–8
DISTINCTIVE FEATURES Rhizome long-creeping, carrying along pinnate-pinnatifid upright blades with nonglandular undersides.
ORIGIN AND HABITAT The New York fern colonizes down the eastern North American seaboard and extends inland brushing midwestern states from Michigan south to Oklahoma. Look for it in moist to wet woodlands, trickling seeps on roadside banks, and swampy muck, usually in acidic soil.
GARDEN AND DESIGN USES Frankly, this fern is too aggressive for most home gardens; however, the light green colonies are refreshing when viewed as a woodland understory or bordering miles of highways. The dual taper of the frond distinguishes it from *T. palustris* and *T. simulata*, whose fronds are widest at their base.

Thelypteris palustris ◂

Marsh fern

TYPE AND SIZE Deciduous, 18–30 inches (45–75 cm) tall
HARDINESS Zones 3–8
DISTINCTIVE FEATURES Rhizome is long and wide-creeping. Lanceolate blades are pinnate-pinnatifid.
ORIGIN AND HABITAT Mainly found tangled among weeds along the margins of lakes and swamps in the eastern United States, as well as in meadows and marshes, this species needs its moisture. It is also native to Europe, the Middle East, and Asia.
GARDEN AND DESIGN USES Marsh fern can be used effectively (on a space-available basis) to soften the contours adjacent to bogs, where it will expand at will in sun or shade.

Thelypteris simulata

Massachusetts fern, bog fern

TYPE AND SIZE Deciduous, 1.5–2.5 feet (45–75 cm) tall

HARDINESS Zones 4–6

DISTINCTIVE FEATURES The rhizome is long-creeping. Lanceolate blades are pinnate-pinnatifid with an undercoating of burnt orange to golden glands and a sparse smattering of hairs.

ORIGIN AND HABITAT The Massachusetts fern enjoys the typical *Thelypteris* surroundings of moist, boggy, and in this case, sphagnum, substrates. Its natural spread, however, is more localized than fellow native thelypteris, with the range confined to eastern Canadian provinces, New England, and disjunct sites in Virginia and Wisconsin.

GARDEN AND DESIGN USES This is a better-mannered *Thelypteris* garden subject not quite so inclined to dominate the landscape. It is best in a wet, peaty, and winter chilly site.

WOODSIA
Cliff fern

Woodsias are small charmers whose early emerging, cheerful green crosiers bring the promise of spring just when winter seems without end. Deciduous and rugged, the majority of the 35 to 45 species are native to temperate climates, frequently alpine, in the Northern Hemisphere.

The genus is named for British architect Joseph Woods (1776–1864). The species typically grow in densely foliated clumps from compact rhizomes. The stipes are sometimes jointed (a diagnostic trait) at their midsection, with fronds falling off cleanly at the break. Significantly, old stipe bases are persistent. Blades tend to be lanceolate or linear and are once-pinnate to bipinnate. Unlike genera with indusia on the top of the sori, woodsias have a star-shaped inferior indusium that sits under the sori and wraps it with fingers somewhat like tentacles of a hydra.

Despite their appearance, woodsias generally prefer exposed rocky habitats and are amazingly sun tolerant. They are popular in gritty niches and screes in rock gardens. Soil preferences vary from basic to acidic, with good drainage a requisite. All the species benefit from a top dressing of rock crumbles to prevent mud from splashing on the foliage. They propagate readily from spores, and after several crowns have formed may easily be increased by division.

Some species, particularly *Woodsia obtusa*, are superficially similar in appearance to species of *Cystopteris*. Both genera are deciduous. The indusia are different, however, with *Cystopteris* sori covered by hooded indusia. Mature *Woodsia* spores are brown, whereas those of *Cystopteris* are black.

Woodsia fragilis
Fragile wood fern

TYPE AND SIZE Deciduous, 6–12 inches (15–30 cm) tall

HARDINESS Zones 5–8

DISTINCTIVE FEATURES Rhizome is short-creeping. Pinnate-pinnatifid to bipinnate blades are lanceolate.

ORIGIN AND HABITAT The fragile wood fern is partial to chinks in rock faces in montane habitats of the Caucasus. Unlike its relatives, its most vigorous populations are on wet limestone, which is neither required nor even welcome in the traditional fern garden.

GARDEN AND DESIGN USES Grow this in well-drained grit. (A trough is excellent.) Once it is established, water at your convenience. *Woodsia fragilis* is one of the easiest of these soft and leafy alpines for traditional garden sites.

Woodsia obtusa
Blunt-lobed woodsia

TYPE AND SIZE Deciduous, 6–16 inches (15–40 cm) tall, sterile fronds may be winter green

HARDINESS Zones 3–8

DISTINCTIVE FEATURES Rhizomes are erect, as are the fronds. Stipes are not jointed. Bipinnate to bipinnate-pinnatifid blades are elliptic, with whitish glands and hairs on both surfaces.

ORIGIN AND HABITAT Noted for its upright habit, *W. obtusa* is equally at home as a vertical in mortared walls or in acidic rock ledges along the east coast of North America.

GARDEN AND DESIGN USES While this species will never make a dramatic statement in the garden design, it is easy to cultivate, especially in cold temperate landscapes.

Woodsia polystichoides
Holly fern woodsia

TYPE AND SIZE Deciduous, 6–14 inches (15–35 cm) tall

HARDINESS Zones 5–8

DISTINCTIVE FEATURES Rhizome is erect to creeping, with tufts of old stipe bases. Stipes are jointed. Narrow, once-pinnate lax blades are linear with a frond outline similar to that of a petite *Polystichum*.

ORIGIN AND HABITAT This choice species is common among exposed rocks in the mountains of Japan, eastern Russia, Korea, China, and Taiwan. A heavily cloaked form from Kamchatka ▶ bears fronds that appear to be almost white under their protective polar coat of hairs and scales.

GARDEN AND DESIGN USES Easily introduced to the partially sunny, fern-forbidding sites of rock gardens, holly fern woodsia cheerfully cascades and meanders among the rocks.

WOODWARDIA
Chain fern

While small, the genus *Woodwardia* includes some remarkably ornamental ferns from stately giants to a pair of eastern American natives adapted to inhospitable swamplands. The 13 or 14 species are named after British botanist Thomas Woodward (1745?–1820). Native primarily to northern temperate zones, these species range from the United States to Costa Rica, the Mediterranean, and eastern Asia. The foliage is characterized by partially netted veins and imbedded linear sori that on most species resemble links of chains or chains of sausages. All species prefer acidic soil. The two eastern American natives, *W. areolata* and *W. virginica*, both deciduous, are noticeably different from the rest of their relatives as well as from one another.

Woodwardia areolata
Netted chain fern

TYPE AND SIZE Deciduous, dimorphic, 1–2 feet (30–60 cm) tall

HARDINESS Zones 3–9

DISTINCTIVE FEATURES Slender long-creeping rhizomes produce sterile fronds to 2 feet (60 cm) tall with oval-triangular pinnatifid blades. The linear pinnae have netted veins. Narrower fertile fronds, which are distinctively winged, arise late in the season.

ORIGIN AND HABITAT *Woodwardia areolata* is primarily a coastal species of eastern North America ranging from Nova Scotia down through Florida and sparingly west. It thrives in shady to partially sunny acidic boggy conditions from water's edge to drainage ditches.

GARDEN AND DESIGN USES This extremely cold tolerant species is a natural choice for boggy areas, where it will happily romp about. The Rhododendron Species Botanical Garden in Federal Way, Washington, has a particularly attractive pondside planting combining swampland ferns with pitcher plants (*Sarracenia*). Netted chain fern does not require marshy soil, but it will be smaller in upland gardens. Although deciduous, the fronds persist well into autumn with warm autumn-colored foliage. Propagation is easy from division as well as spores. The species is sometimes confused with the superficially similar *Onoclea sensibilis*. However, on the latter, the lowermost pinnae are not winged, and the fertile fronds consist of brown beadlike segments.

Woodwardia fimbriata

Giant chain fern

TYPE AND SIZE Evergreen, 4–8 feet (1.2–2.4 m) tall

HARDINESS Zones 8–10

DISTINCTIVE FEATURES This statuesque fern grows from a stout and ascending rhizome. It is a stately clump with tall arching fronds to 4 feet (1.2 m) at the northern end of its range and closer to 8 feet (2.4 m) in California's redwood forests. The coarse, dark green, pinnate-pinnatifid blade is lanceolate. The chains of sori are prominently visible on the upper surface of the frond. Note that the new growth is not red-toned nor does the frond sport a bulbil.

ORIGIN AND HABITAT The giant chain fern is a coastal species that grows in moist coniferous woodlands from a few rare stations in British Columbia down through southern California. It is especially common and impressive in the redwood forests.

GARDEN AND DESIGN USES Where suited, this is an extremely showy specimen well deserving of a prominent place in the landscape. In cold winters, it will need pampering when temperatures drop below 20°F (–7°C).

Woodwardia orientalis
Oriental chain fern

TYPE AND SIZE Evergreen, 3–5 feet (0.9–1.5 m) tall or taller

HARDINESS Zones (8 with protection) 9 and 10

DISTINCTIVE FEATURES The scaly, short, ascending rhizome gives rise to a vase of bright green ovate fronds. The blade, like many woodwardias, is pinnate-pinnatifid with pointed toothy pinnae. A mature frond produces an astonishing number of little ready-to-root plantlets, suggestive of tiny Japanese maple seeds (samaras), on the upper surface. These are directly above the soral location and inhibit the growth of the sorus. Without these, the sori develop in the typical chainlike fashion.

ORIGIN AND HABITAT This is native to the forests of Japan, China, Taiwan, the Himalayas, and the Philippines.

GARDEN AND DESIGN USES Zone 8 gardeners may want to keep their plants in an unheated greenhouse during the winter, but this fern is excellent in warm areas, including heated greenhouses. Fronds heavily dressed in plantlets tend to droop, so basket culture is ideal. Wherever grown, the fertile plants are certain to be a conversation piece. Propagation is easily achieved by sitting the little plantlets on compost in a 4-inch (10-cm) pot, covered with a clear plastic cup and put in good light but not direct sunlight. Give some away. A crested form is more compact, at 18–24 inches (45–60 cm), and has crests on the tips of the fronds.

Woodwardia radicans ▸

European chain fern

TYPE AND SIZE Evergreen, 2–6 feet (60–180 cm) tall
HARDINESS Zones 9–10
DISTINCTIVE FEATURES The stout ascending rhizome supports vigorously tall fronds with ovate-lanceolate, pinnate-pinnatifid blades. The tips of the fronds sport one to several bulbils.
ORIGIN AND HABITAT *Woodwardia radicans* grows in moist partial shade near streams and at the edges of woodlands in southern Europe. In the United States, it has escaped in Florida and California.
GARDEN AND DESIGN USES With its imposing architectural fronds, this species is popular in mild climates as well as being frequently displayed in conservatories, where it enjoys the humidity and puts on a dramatic show.

Woodwardia unigemmata ◂

Jeweled chain fern

TYPE AND SIZE Evergreen, 3–6 feet (0.9–1.8 m) tall
HARDINESS Zones 8–10
DISTINCTIVE FEATURES A thick rhizome produces fountains of cascading foliage. Young fronds are a sumptuous sight of glossy red. A bulbil, in some cases several, forms at the tip of each frond and will reproduce when pinned down on suitable soil.
ORIGIN AND HABITAT This jewel is a colonizer of mountain forests from Japan, China, and the Himalayas to the Philippines. An attractive undulate variety is being grown in Britain.
GARDEN AND DESIGN USES This gem of the genus provides a rosy draping skirt of up to 6 feet (1.8 m). Display plants at the top of a wall or on a hillside where the fronds can flow downward in a showy effort to plant their bulbils. This species has survived winter temperatures of 14°F (−10°C), but when necessary it can be protected with a blanket of light horticultural gauze.

Woodwardia virginica

Virginia chain fern

TYPE AND SIZE Deciduous, 1–3 feet (30–90 cm) tall

HARDINESS Zones 3–9

DISTINCTIVE FEATURES Erect fronds emerge from along a coarse, long-creeping and branching rhizome that frequently grows in mud or even under water. The narrowly ovate blade is pinnate-pinnatifid with mustard-colored new growth.

ORIGIN AND HABITAT This is primarily a colonizing fern of partially shaded acidic swamps, bogs, and marshes in the coastal areas of Canada and the entire eastern seaboard of the United States as well as Bermuda.

GARDEN AND DESIGN USES Handsome and garden worthy, *W. virginica* will migrate freely and somewhat aggressively in wet spongy areas. It is a logical choice where such a cover is welcome. In wet areas, it can take full sun. Conversely, with reports that rhizomes may be about 10 feet (3 m) long, you may want to consider containing garden plantings. For drier fern beds, choose another plant or water this one liberally. The species is quite unlike other chain ferns, but sterile fronds may sometimes be confused with those of *Osmundastrum cinnamomeum*. Fronds arranged in a symmetrical crown rather than in randomly scattered growth easily distinguish the latter.

GROWING
AND
PROPAGATING

M

Most ferns are easy to grow and thrive in average garden situations, as long as they are not exposed to hot sun or excessively dry conditions. Ferns prefer locations in bright to medium shade or in areas with dappled light, and humus-rich soil with adequate drainage where they will not have wet feet. Plant ferns when temperatures are not too hot and the ground is not frozen. In areas with extremes in weather, it is best to plant in spring or early autumn.

Soak ferns that are to be planted in a bucket the day before to make sure the rootball is thoroughly moistened. Remove the fern from its pot, and gently loosen the roots. Dig a hole about the same depth as the rootball and at least three times the width. Plant the fern so that the base of the crown (the growing point of a stem) is even with the surrounding soil. Gently firm the soil around the rootball, but do not pack it down. Ferns like an open and light soil structure, and the roots will establish more quickly with a gentle firming of the soil. Water the newly planted fern thoroughly. Apply 1 to 2 inches (2.5–5 cm) of mulch around the ferns, which will help maintain the soil moisture, keep the roots cool in the summer, and offer protection in winter.

Regular watering will be necessary for at least the first year until the root system is well established. Once established, mature ferns may only need watering during prolonged drought or excessively hot weather. A slow trickle of water is best when watering, to allow the water to penetrate the soil deeply. The length and frequency of watering will vary depending on climate and soil conditions. Soaker hoses and drip irrigation may be helpful to keep plants watered and make the best use of this limited resource.

Well-grown specimens of *Adiantum aleuticum* and *Athyrium niponicum* 'Applecourt'.

A graveyard with ferns in Salzburg, Austria.

Dealing with Problem Soils

Although ferns prefer soil rich in organic matter, they will tolerate far less ideal sites. Gardens with sand, clay, or heavily compacted soils can also enjoy ferns with a little planning. Start by looking for ferns that will tolerate your particular soil conditions.

Sandy soils benefit from the addition of organic matter, which will help to hold moisture and nutrients as the fern establishes. Water sandy soils deeply and infrequently to encourage a deep drought-tolerant root system. Applying mulch will help maintain the moisture in these well-draining situations.

Organic matter will also help ferns establish in clay soils. Coarse organic matter, such as compost, with the addition of gypsum worked into the soil will help open air space for roots to grow. If the soils are particularly heavy, plant the ferns slightly higher than the surrounding soils and mound the soil up to the crown. Mulching will help prevent the soil from cracking in dry weather, which could damage the new roots of an establishing fern.

Urban gardens can suffer from heavily compacted soils, which may not drain well. To check the drainage in your soil, fill a hole with water to see how long it takes it to drain out. If it is more than a few minutes, you should consider planting in a raised bed.

A bed with a 6-inch (15-cm) depth will accommodate most ferns (although it may need to be deeper for other plants). Several tough ferns will tolerate compacted soil conditions. Dig the hole wide and shallow. Loosen the soil, and add organic matter and grit to help keep the soil loose until the fern establishes over the next couple of years. Plant the fern so that the base is slightly higher than the surrounding soil, and then mound up to the base with soil.

Watering and Fertilizing

Watering needs vary depending on the fern being grown. Most ferns prefer weekly watering during the growing season, although most will survive short periods of drought. If additional watering cannot be supplied once ferns have become established in an area, plant drought-tolerant species. Keep in mind that drought-tolerant ferns may survive with little additional watering, but after a few weeks of dry conditions during the growing season they will begin to suffer.

Established ferns do not need regular fertilizing to maintain an attractive appearance or have robust growth. Many will grow perfectly fine with little more than regular watering. Established ferns or ferns showing yellow green fronds may benefit from an application of an all-purpose fertilizer. Organic fertilizer can be helpful due to the slow release of nutrients over a long time. Newly planted ferns generally will not need fertilizing for the first year.

Pruning

Yearly removal of old fronds provides a crisp clean appearance in the landscape. Deciduous ferns can be cut to the ground in autumn once the foliage begins to turn yellow. Some ferns have attractive autumn color, however, and these can be cut to the ground once they have become brown.

Evergreen ferns can be cut down once a year, but this is not necessary for the health of the plant. Because evergreen ferns photosynthesize over the winter, leaving the foliage for most of the winter protects the crown from severe freezing and promotes robust growth in the spring. Winter-growing species of *Polypodium* produce a new flush of foliage from

Ferns for Dry Shade

Dryopteris affinis and cultivars
Dryopteris dilatata and cultivars
Dryopteris erythrosora
Dryopteris filix-mas and cultivars
Dryopteris formosana
Dryopteris remota
Polypodium scouleri
Polystichum acrostichoides
Polystichum munitum
Polystichum setiferum

Ferns for Sunny Locations

THESE TOLERATE SUN within reason, but many will not take hot midday sun and require regular watering.

Asplenium trichomanes
Athyrium filix-femina
Blechnum penna-marina
Ceterach officinarum
Cheilanthes spp.
Dennstaedtia punctilobula
Dryopteris affinis and cultivars
Dryopteris ×complexa

Xeric Ferns

DRYLAND FERNS ARE not for beginners. For those who wish to begin, however, the following are easier—not to be confused with easy. These ferns are suitable for Zone 7 and warmer, with some suitable for Zone 6.

Astrolepis sinuata
Cheilanthes eatonii
Cheilanthes fendleri
Cheilanthes lanosa
Cheilanthes lindheimeri
Cheilanthes tomentosa
Cheilanthes wootonii
Pellaea atropurpurea

Fading foliage of a *Polypodium* with fresh fronds emerging.

Ferns That Should Not Be Cut Back in Winter

IN ADDITION TO these ferns, avoid cutting back dwarf and slow-growing evergreen species and cultivars.

Aleuritopteris argentea
Arachniodes (especially in areas with cool summers)
Asplenium trichomanes
Blechnum chilense
Cheilanthes (all species)
Dryopteris bissetiana
Dryopteris sieboldii
Pellaea (all species)
Polypodium
Pyrrosia (all species and cultivars)
Rumohra (especially in areas with cool summers)
Woodwardia (all evergreen species)

late summer to autumn. Watch for yellowing foliage in late spring or early summer. They can be cut back once the foliage yellows or periodically groomed as the fronds die.

Most evergreen ferns can be cut back in late winter to early spring, prior to the new crosiers emerging. Even if the old fronds look perfectly fine, it is best to remove them all before the new growth emerges. Once new fronds emerge, old fronds will begin to deteriorate and can look unsightly through the spring. There are some exceptions to this rule of pruning ferns in early spring. Some evergreen ferns flop in early to mid-winter. After a few heavy rains or a snow, the fronds bend at the base and fall around the crown. The old fronds of these ferns can be removed once they have fallen or are no longer attractive.

Some evergreen ferns, however, are weakened when cut back in late winter; therefore, old fronds should be removed only when they begin to yellow and die. This is especially true for dwarf and slow-growing species and cultivars. Unfortunately, only experience will make clear which evergreen ferns should not be pruned.

Growing Ferns in Containers

Container gardening is a mainstay of the urban landscape. Ferns are well adapted to life in a pot and can be a perfect means of gardening for the pteridophile without much room. Ferns are especially useful for containers in shady locations, with evergreen species being assets nearly all year long.

A garden container can be almost anything that will hold soil and has drainage holes. When choosing a container, consider its purpose in the garden, which can range from serving as a focal point to helping to screen or conceal unwanted views. Choose a container and plants that help accomplish this purpose. Containers should be large enough to accommodate root growth adequately, the smaller the pot, the more often it will need watering. Pots made from porous material like terracotta will dry out faster than plastic, resin, or glazed ceramic containers. Locate containers so that they can be watered easily and efficiently. Protect ferns from windy locations, strong winds can break and dry out fronds.

Soil mixes vary depending on what is being planted, the size of the container, how long the plants are expected to grow in the container, and the climate in which you are gardening. Local gardeners and nurseries can be helpful in selecting the appropriate soil mix. However, a few considerations are universal. Avoid mixes with topsoil. Topsoil is great for gardening, but it is too dense and lacks the pore space needed to grow ferns well in a container. Avoid mixes with a high peat moss content unless the ferns will be transplanted in less than two years. Peat moss breaks down quickly and can become wet muck after a year or so. Plants potted in peat moss will initially grow well, but will decline in vigor over time. Soil mixes with combinations of coarse compost, bark, pumice, perlite, or gravel can provide a rich, but well-aerated growing medium for

Specimen ferns in a large container.

ferns. Coarse grades of sand can also be used, but avoid fine grades commonly found in sandbox or play sand. These coarse open mixes can allow for optimum growth for three to five years.

MIXED CONTAINER DESIGN

A well-composed container captures the essence of a garden on a miniature scale. Appealing containers are creative in the use of texture, color, and form. Cliché as it is, the overused phrase "thrillers, fillers, and spillers" does create a beautiful container composition. The thrillers are tall and dramatic plants, the fillers are mostly rounded and mounded forms, and the spillers are plants that flow over the edge of the container. A good container combines these three plant forms with interesting and contrasting textures and colors. For each container, however, it is important to select plants that all enjoy the same growing conditions.

Strong textural contrasts, such as mixing fine textures with bold leaves, catch the eye and draw attention. The small bright green leaflets of *Adiantum venustum* (Himalayan maidenhair) make the large angular leaflets of *Cyrtomium macrophyllum* (bigleaf

Creative placement
of containers in
the Goulding gar-
den in the United
Kingdom.

holly fern) stand out even more than usual. Using similar textures together softens the visual draw and provides a calming quality. Using *A. venustum* surrounding the taller, upright and similarly textured *Athyrium filix-femina* 'Lady in Red' (red-stemmed northern lady fern) creates an elegant, yet beautiful container. Experimenting with different ferns and textures will help you learn what combinations you like best. Containers are temporary. If you do not like a planting combination, remove the offending plants and replace.

CONTAINER MAINTENANCE

Ferns are easy, low-maintenance container plants. They do not need deadheading and won't become a slimy mess at the first frost. Container-grown ferns need little in the way of grooming. Deciduous ferns can be cut down when the fronds turn yellow in autumn. The fronds of evergreen ferns should be cut to the base in late winter to early spring. Any broken or damaged fronds can be removed as noticed.

The only critical needs of container-grown ferns are water and a little fertilizer. All potted ferns need regular watering during the growing season. If the container is under cover, it will need some watering even in the winter. Water should be added until it runs out the bottom drainage holes. Saucers can be placed below smaller containers to help hold some water during hot weather. If the container dries out completely, rewetting the soil can be difficult. A small container can be placed in a bucket for an hour or two to saturate the soil. Larger containers will need several waterings spaced a few hours apart to rehydrate the soil or a very light dribble from a hose can be left on the soil surface for a few hours.

Container-grown ferns need regular fertilizing. A slow-release granular material applied in spring can keep the plants healthy and dark green through the entire growing season. Organic fertilizers can provide similar long-term results. Sometimes organic fertilizers can mold as part of their natural decomposing process. To prevent this, bury them under the top layer of soil or apply a light layer of mulch. Liquid fertilizers are quite effective for containers, but must be applied regularly. Liquid fertilizers can also give a nice boost in late summer if slow-release materials have lost their effectiveness.

Tall and Dramatic Ferns (Thrillers)

Adiantum aleuticum (or *A. pedatum*)
Coniogramme intermedia
Dicksonia antarctica
Dryopteris affinis 'Cristata'
Dryopteris ×complexa 'Stableri Crisped'
Dryopteris filix-mas 'Barnesii'
Osmunda regalis
Osmundastrum cinnamomeum
Polystichum ×dycei
Polystichum munitum
Woodwardia unigemmata

Rounded and Mounded Ferns (Fillers)

Asplenium scolopendrium
Athyrium otophorum
Cyrtomium falcatum
Dryopteris cycadina
Dryopteris erythrosora
Polystichum aculeatum
Polystichum neolobatum
Polystichum polyblepharum

Draping Ferns (Spillers)

Athyrium niponicum 'Pictum'
Polypodium scouleri
Polypodium vulgare
Polystichum setiferum Divisilobum Group
Polystichum setiferum Plumosomultilobum Group
Pyrrosia lingua

An expertly planted trough with xeric ferns.

WINTER CARE

Winter care will depend on the type of container and the plants selected. Plants that are not tolerant of heavy freezes should be removed from containers and heeled in the ground for the winter, and the containers should be cleaned and stored in a dry place. Frost-resistant plants can remain in containers all year long. The roots of container plants are exposed to greater temperature extremes than if they were grown in the ground. Parts of a plant that are above the soil line tend to be hardier than the roots, and quick cold snaps and rapid fluctuations in temperatures can harm the more delicate roots. When choosing ferns for containers, plant ferns that are suited to areas at least one or two hardiness zones colder than your zone, especially in areas where the winter temperatures can drop below 10°F (–12°C). Reducing fertilizing and watering in autumn can also help ferns harden off for winter temperatures.

TROUGHS

A great way to enjoy alpine and xeric species of ferns is to grow them in troughs. These are generally long low containers made of stone, ceramic, or hypertufa (a homemade concrete mix). If the trough does not have drainage holes, a large masonry drill can easily remedy the problem. To grow well, ferns need a minimum soil depth of 6 inches (15 cm), preferably 8 to 12 inches (20–30 cm). Use a very well-draining soil mix, such as 3 parts very coarse sand, 2 parts gravel or pumice, and 1 part coarse compost. Find interesting rocks and sculptural pieces of wood to add interesting accents, then tuck ferns around and accent with other alpines, dwarf conifers, or dryland plants with similar care needs. Find a place with bright light, but no hot sun. Place the trough slightly elevated on top of bricks to keep worms from crawling into the drainage holes. Worm castings clog the drainage holes and can ruin the open soil structure.

Pests and Diseases

Ferns are relatively problem free. The few pests or diseases that can inflict ferns are rarely severe. Most can be controlled through good cultural practices with minimal need for pesticides.

APHIDS (GREENFLY OR BLACKFLY)

These small soft-bodied insects, also called greenflies or blackflies, come in many colors, including the more common green and black as well as yellow and pink. They prefer soft succulent growth and can cause damage from feeding on newly emerging crosiers. As the fronds unfurl, they develop contorted, deformed growth. Minor injury can show as a yellow somewhat circular spot on the leaf. Often, by the time the damage is noticed, the aphids have moved on. Look for tiny teardrop-shaped insects on newly emerging fronds, the underside of the leaf, or near the base of the leaf stem. Control is rarely necessary. Aphids will generally only feed on ferns for short periods during the lushness of growth. Damaged fronds noticed later in the season can be removed if unsightly. Aphids warrant control only if the population is particularly heavy or regularly reoccurring.

LEAF-ROLLER CATERPILLARS

This minor pest can cause very noticeable damage. As the new fern fronds emerge, the industrious caterpillar gathers the leaflets and rolls them into a bundle, where it feeds and develops until it becomes a moth. The best control is to simply pick off the caterpillar with its leaf bundled house and dispose of properly (meaning squash it underfoot).

Leafroller on *Dryopteris dilatata*

Leafhoppers' Favorite Ferns

Dryopteris affinis and cultivars
Dryopteris ×*complexa*
Dryopteris dilatata and cultivars
Dryopteris filix-mas and cultivars
Polypodium cambricum (when grown in sun)
Polypodium ×*mantoniae* (when grown in sun)
Polypodium vulgare (when grown in sun)

Watch for slime trails!

LEAFHOPPERS

Leafhoppers are annoying but will not kill a fern. They disfigure the appearance by peppering the foliage with small yellowish white spots. Heavy infestations can make a plant unsightly by the late summer, draining the color to that of a cheap bleach job. Leafhoppers are small, narrow, wedge-shaped insects that are generally pale greenish white. They are quick flying and sometimes confused with whitefly, but leafhoppers are larger and fly with greater purpose and speed. Brushing against a heavily infested plant in late summer will invite a brief explosion of speedy flight.

Spraying can kill the natural predators of leafhoppers and cause a population explosion of the offending insect. Only spray if there is a heavy infestation. Several low-toxicity and organic pesticides will subdue leafhoppers, but all must come in contact with the insect. If you choose to spray, the pesticide must thoroughly cover the undersides of the foliage to be effective. Only a few ferns are particularly susceptible. Avoid these species if leafhoppers are a serious problem in your garden.

SLUGS AND SNAILS

Garden mollusks can quickly mow down and shred the fronds of their favorite ferns. Fortunately, most ferns are not to their liking. If mollusks insist on eating a plant or two in your garden, there is a wealth of pellet baits that do a great job of control. Occasionally, snails will reside in the fronds out of reach of the tempting baits. Hand picking and dropping into a jar of soapy water or enjoying the satisfying crunch under the boot heel offers excellent control.

VINE WEEVILS AND ROOT WEEVILS

Vine weevils and root weevils are black or mottled brown and have the distinctive long snout of all weevils. The adults chew small notches along the edges of fronds, and heavy infestations can make the fern unattractive. Ferns are not their preferred food and are typically near plants more favored by this pest. The larva, a small white grub, can cause considerable damage in container plants. The larva feed on roots and can kill potted plants. The damage occurs from late autumn to late spring. If a plant looks lackluster in late winter and seems loose in the pot, remove the ferns and examine the soil. The grubs can be picked out and destroyed. Local nurseries or the Cooperative Extension Service can provide advice on weevil control.

DEER AND RABBITS

Ferns seem to have at least partial resistance to the feeding of deer, but rabbits view ferns as a growing salad bar. The tastes of both of these pests can vary from region to region and from year to year. Both deer and rabbits can be difficult to control without well-thought-out fencing. Repellent sprays can offer some relief, but they must be used early in the season to protect new growth and reapplied regularly, especially in the case of rabbits. As evergreen fern fronds mature, the tougher texture is sometimes less appealing. A little experimenting and observation will let you know if you need to apply repellents for the entire season. Those who can tolerate the cycle of life can encourage natural and domestic predators. The family dog can earn its keep by patrolling the perimeter of the fern garden. Their regular presence alone can be an effective deterrent to these cute, yet destructive animals.

FOLIAGE DISEASES AND ROOT ROTS

Foliage diseases and root rots are uncommon among ferns and are mostly associated with growing conditions that are less than ideal.

To treat foliar diseases, improve the air circulation around the plant and avoid keeping the foliage wet for long periods. Watering in the morning will allow the fronds to dry during the day. Moving the fern to a more open location may also help. Remove any infected fronds and dispose of them in the garbage. Do not compost infected foliage or plants. Root rot is a sure sign of the soil staying too wet. Infected ferns are best disposed of in the garbage. Use ferns that tolerate wet conditions, these are naturally resistant to root rot.

JAPANESE HOLLY FERN MOTTLE VIRUS

This recently identified virus causes yellow mottling, spotting, and ringlike patterns on the fronds of *Cyrtomium*, in particular *Cyrtomium falcatum*, Japanese holly fern. Infected plants look unsightly and gradually decline in vigor. This virus may be spread by sucking insects, but more research is needed to confirm this. There is no cure for this virus, and infected plants should be removed immediately and destroyed. Do not compost infected ferns. This is the first known virus to be spread by spore, so it is also important not to propagate using spore collected from infected plants.

Propagation

Gardeners can propagate ferns by three means: division, rooting bulbils, and sowing spore. Division and bulbil production will give plants that look identical to the parent plant, whereas spore-grown fern can be variable.

The symptoms of Japanese holly fern mottle virus are variable in appearance. Destroy infected plants.

DIVISION

Division is the best method for slowly spreading and groundcover ferns and those with several crowns. Division is most successful when the fern is dormant, the weather is cool, and the soil is moist. Groundcover and spreading ferns can be cut into clumps with a spade and placed into a new location. Deciduous groundcover ferns can nearly be bare rooted during this process and be successfully moved. Although evergreen groundcover ferns may tolerate bare rooting, it will slow their reestablishment. Clumping ferns with several crowns can be divided using a sharp tool. Cut away a full crown with roots and pot it in compost. Keep it well watered until established and ready for the garden. Another method is to dig the entire parent plant, tease apart the roots, and then perform surgery.

BULBILS

Some ferns, especially *Polystichum setiferum* cultivars and a few *Woodwardia* species, produce bulbils along the rachis (frond stem) or at the tip. Bulbils are buds (small bulb-like growths) that will produce new plants if allowed to root and grow.

A simple method of propagating is to pin down the frond on the surrounding soil while still attached to the parent. This can be done from autumn to late winter. By the following growing season at least a few of the bulbils will have rooted.

Fronds can also be removed and incubated on the soil surface in a humid enclosure. A small pot covered by an inverted clear plastic cup placed in good light but not direct sun will work.

The fronds can also be moistened and placed in a sealed plastic bag. Place the bag in good light but not direct sun. In about one or two months, the bulbils will have sprouted new fronds and roots and can be plucked from the stem and placed in soil in a humid enclosure.

Mature bulbils of *Polystichum setiferum* Rotundatum Group are ready to root.

GROWING FROM SPORE

Eventually, however, the truly addicted want the pleasure of propagating ferns from spore. Because ferns don't have flowers and seeds, they are propagated from dustlike spores. These are usually found on the undersides of the frond and ripen from mid to late summer. Harvesting may bring a dropping of chaff as well as spores, so clean by placing the entire crop on a white piece of paper, tip, and gently tap. The chaff will roll away, and the fine powdery dust that remains is spore.

There are as many preferred options for a sowing medium as there are propagators. Preferences range from peat-based soils and earthworm compost to customized mixes. Whatever the choice, it is best to pasteurize the selected medium. Moisten, cover lightly, and heat it in an oven for three hours at 175°F (80°C). Place the cooled mix into a clear container, moisten, lightly dust with spores, place in good light, and wait. Ideally, in time a green coating of little heart-shaped growths that are the ferns' intermediate stage will develop. Mist the culture gently and, if all goes well, sporelings (very young ferns just emerging from spores) will develop. When this promising culture becomes crowded, separate the sporelings as plugs and transplant them into slightly larger containers while still maintaining humidity. When the progeny are several inches tall, harden them off and transplant into individual pots. This entire procedure takes months, but the reward is well worth the wait.

Dustlike fertile green spores of *Osmundastrum cinnamomeum*

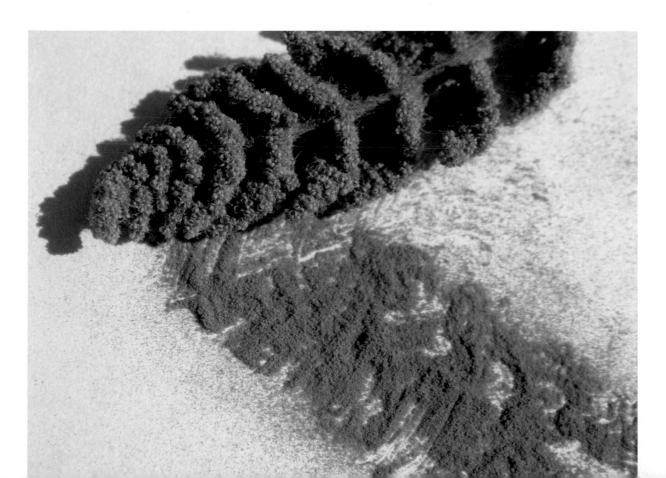

WHERE TO BUY

CANADA

Pacific Rim Native Plant Nursery
P.O. Box 413
Chilliwack
British Columbia V2P 6J7
www.hillkeep.ca

Thimble Farms Nursery
175 Arbutus Road
Salt Spring Island
British Columbia V8K 1A3
www.thimblefarms.com

ENGLAND

Bowden
Cleave House
Sticklepat
Okehampton
Devon EX20 2NL
www.bowdenhostas.com

Fernatix
Honington
Suffolk IP31 1QY
www.fernatix.co.uk

The Fern Nursery
R. N. Timm
Grimsby Road
Binbrook
Lincolnshire LN8 6DH
www.fernnursery.co.uk

Fibrex Nurseries
Honeybourne Road
Pebworth
Stratford-upon-Avon
Warwickshire CV37 8XP
www.fibrex.co.uk

Ivycroft Plants
Ivington Green
Leominster HR6 0JN
www.ivycroftgarden.co.uk

Pan-Global Plants
The Walled Garden
Frampton Court
Gloucester GL2 7EX
www.panglobalplants.com

FRANCE

Fougères d'ici & d'ailleurs
La Bricole FR 40310
www.fougeresdicietdailleurs.com

Le Monde des Fougères
955 Chemin de Puits
Roquefort Les Pins 06330
www.pepinieres-ezavin.com

GERMANY

Stauden Junge
Seeangerweg 1
31787 Hameln
www.stauden-junge.de

IRELAND

Dicksonia Direct
28 Mount Eagle Rise
Leopardstown Heights
Dublin, 18

Shady Plants Fern Nursery
Coolbooa
Clashmore
County Waterford
www.shadyplants.net

UNITED STATES

Cady's Falls Nursery
637 Duhamel Road
Morrisville, Vermont 05661
www.cadysfallsnurery.com
No mail order.

Charles Alford Plants
Vero Beach, Florida 32962
www.rareferns.com
Mail order only.

Fancy Fronds Nursery
P.O. Box 1090
Gold Bar, Washington 98251
www.fancyfronds.com

Far Reaches Farm
1818 Hastings Avenue
Port Townsend, Washington 98368
www.farreachesfarm.com

The Fern Factory
1201 North Andrea Lane
Anaheim, California 92807
www.fernfactory.com

Fern Ridge Farms
6254 Highway 273
Cedar Bluff, Alabama 35959
www.fernridgefarms.com

Foliage Gardens
2003 128th Avenue SE
Bellevue, Washington 98005
www.foliagegardens.com
Visitors by appointment.

Forest Farm
990 Tethrow Road
Williams, Oregon 97544
www.forestfarm.com

Glasshouse Works
Church Street
P.O. Box 97
Stewart, Ohio 45778
www.glasshouseworks.com

Hardy Fern Foundation
2525 S 336th Street
Federal Way, Washington 98003
www.hardyferns.org

Keeping It Green Nursery
19401 96th Avenue NW
Stanwood, Washington 98292
www.keepingitgreennursery.com
Best to make an appointment.

Plant Delights Nursery
9241 Sauls Road
Raleigh, North Carolina 27603
www.plantdelights.com
Visitors by appointment.

Sundquist Nursery
3809 NE Sawdust Hill Road
Poulsbo, Washington 98370
www.sqnursery.com
See website for open garden days.

WALES

Aberconwy Nursery
Graig
Glan Conwy LL28 5TL
01492 580875

WHERE TO SEE

Adelaide Botanic Garden
North Terrace
Adelaide, South Australia 5000
www.environment.sa.gov.au/
botanicgardens/adelaide.html

Brisbane Botanic Garden
Mount Coot-tha Road
Toowong, Queensland 4066
www.brisbane.qld.gov.au/botanicgardens

Mount Lofty Botanic Garden
Summit Road
Crafers, South Australia 5152
www.environment.sa.gov.
au/botanicgardens/visit/
mount_lofty_botanic_garden

Royal Botanic Garden, Melbourne
Birdwood Avenue
South Yarra, Victoria 3141
www.rbg.vic.gov.au

Royal Botanic Garden, Sydney
Mrs. MacQuaries Road
Sydney, New South Wales 2000
www.sydney.com.au/rbg.htm

CANADA

Le Jardin Botanique de Montréal
4101 Sherbrooke Est
Montreal, Québec H1X 2B2
espacepourlavie.ca/jardin-botanique

Les Jardins de Métis
200, Route 132
Grand-Métis, Québec G0J 1Z0
www.jardinsmetis.com

Van Dusen Botanical Garden
5251 Oak Street
Vancouver, British Columbia V6M 4H1
www.vandusengarden.org

ENGLAND

Biddulph Grange Garden
Grange Road
Biddulph, Stoke-on-Trent ST8 7SD
www.nationaltrust.org.uk/
biddulph-grange-garden

Brodsworth Hall and Gardens
Doncaster
West Yorkshire DN5 7XJ
www.english-heritage.org.uk/daysout/
properties/brodsworth-hall-and-gardens

Cambridge University Botanic Gardens
1 Brookside
Cambridge CB2 1JF
www.botanic.cam.ac.uk

Chelsea Physic Garden
66 Royal Hospital Road
London SW3 4HS
www.chelseaphysicgarden.co.uk

Harlow Carr Botanic Gardens
(Northern Horticultural Society)
Crag Lane
Harrogate
North Yorkshire HG3 1UE
www.rhs.org.uk/WhatsOn/gardens/
harlowcarr/index.asp

RHS Garden Wisley
Wisley Lane
Wisley
Woking GU23 6QB
www.rhs.org.uk/gardens/wisley

Royal Botanic Gardens Kew
Richmond
Surrey TW9 3AB
www.rbgkew.org.uk

Savill Garden
(part of Windsor Great Park)
Wick Lane, Englefield Green
Egham, Surrey TW20 0UU
www.theroyallandscape.co.uk/
gardens-and-landscape/the-savill-garden
*Holder of the National Collection of Hardy
Ferns.*

Sizergh Castle and Garden
Kendal, Cumbria LA8 8AE
www.visitcumbria.com/sl/sizergh.htm
A National Trust garden.

Southport Botanic Gardens
Bankfield Lane
Churchtown, Southport
Merseyside PR9 7NB
www.visitsouthport.com/things-to-do/
botanic-gardens-p56922

Tatton Park
Knutsford, Cheshire WA16 6QN
www.tattonpark.org.uk

Tremenheere Sculpture Gardens
Near Gulval
Penzance, Cornwall TR20 8YL
www.tremenheere.co.uk

University of Oxford Botanic Garden
Rose Lane
Oxford OX1 4DU
www.botanic-garden.ox.ac.uk

FRANCE

Jardin Botanique de Lyon
69205 Lyon Cedex 01
Lyon
www.jardin-botanique-lyon.com

Parc Phoenix-Nice
405, Promenade des Anglais
Nice, Côte d'Azur
www.parc-phoenix.org

GERMANY

Arktisch-Alpiner Garten
Schmidt-Rottluff Strasse
09114 Chemnitz, Saxony
www.arktisch-alpiner-garten.de

Botanischer Garten und Museum
Museum Berlin-Dahlem
Freie Universität Berlin
Königin-Luise-Straße 6-8
14195 Berlin
www.bgbm.org

Flora und Botanischer Garten Köln
Amsterdamer Straße 34
50735 Köln
www.stadt-koeln.de/6/gruen/flora

IRELAND

Caher Bridge Garden
Fanore
County Clare
www.ireland-guide.com/gardens/caher-
bridge-garden.8140.html
By appointment.

Kells Bay Gardens
Kells House
Kells
County Kerry
www.kellsgardens.ie

NETHERLANDS

Hortus Botanicus Leiden
Rapenburg 73
2311 GJ Leiden
www.hortusleiden.nl

NEW ZEALAND

Franz Fernery at the Auckland Domain Park
Auckland 1001
North Island
www.auckland.world-guides.com/
auckland_parks_gardens.html

Pukeiti Rhododendron Trust Garden
2290 Carrington Road
R.D. 4
Pukeiti, New Plymouth 4374
www.pukeiti.org.nz

Pukekura Park
Liardet Street
Brooklands, New Plymouth 4310
www.newplymouthnz.com/OurDistrict/
Attractions/pukekurapark.htm

SCOTLAND

Arduaine Garden
Arduaine, Oban
Argyll PA34 4XQ
www.nts.org.uk/property/arduaine-garden

Ascog Hall Gardens and Victorian Fernery
Isle of Bute
Argyll PA20 9EU
www.greatbritishgardens.co.uk/ascog_
fernery.htm

Attadale Gardens
Attadale, Strathcarron
Wester Ross IV54 8YX
www.attadalegardens.com

Benmore Botanic Garden
Dunoon, Argyll PA23 8QU
www.rbge.org.uk/the-gardens/benmore

Glasgow Botanic Gardens
730 Great Western Road
Glasgow G12 0UE
www.clyde-valley.com/glasgow/botanic.
htm
Holder of the National Collection of the Dicksoniaceae (tree ferns).

Inverewe Garden and Estate
By Poolewe IV22 2LG
www.nts.org.uk/Property/
Inverewe-Garden-and-Estate

Linn Botanic Gardens
Cove, by Helensburgh G84 0NR
www.linnbotanicgardens.org.uk

Logan Botanic Gardens
Port Logan, Stranraer
Wigtownshir, DG9 9ND
www.rbge.org.uk/logan

Royal Botanic Garden Edinburgh
Inverleith Row
Edinburgh EH3 5LR
www.rbge.org.uk

UNITED STATES

Atlanta Botanical Garden
1345 Piedmont Avenue
Atlanta, Georgia 30309
www.atlantabotanicalgarden.org

Balboa Park
2125 Park Blvd.
San Diego, California 92101
www.balboapark.org

Barnes Foundation Arboretum
300 N Latch's Lane
Merion, Pennsylvania 19066
www.barnesfoundation.org

Bartholomew's Cobble
105 Weatogue Road
Ashley Falls, Massachusetts 01222
www.thetrustees.org/places-to-visit/
berkshires/bartholomews-cobble.html

Bellevue Botanical Garden
12001 Main Street
Bellevue, Washington 98005
www.bellevuebotanical.org

Berkshire Botanical Garden
Routes 102 and 183
Stockbridge, Massachusetts 01262
www.berkshirebotanical.org

Birmingham Botanical Garden
2612 Lane Park Road
Birmingham, Alabama 35223
www.bbgardens.org

Bloedel Reserve
7571 NE Dolphin Drive
Bainbridge Island, Washington 98110
www.bloedelreserve.org

Bok Tower Gardens
1151 Tower Gardens
Lake Wales, Florida 33853
www.boksanctuary.org

Botanical Gardens at Asheville
151 W. T. Weaver Blvd.
Asheville, North Carolina 28804
www.ashevillebotanicalgardens.org

Bowman's Hill Wildflower Preserve
1635 River Road
New Hope, Pennsylvania 18938
www.bhwp.org

Brooklyn Botanic Garden
1000 Washington Avenue
Brooklyn, New York 11225
www.bbg.org

**California State University
at Sacramento**
Department of Biology
6000 J Street
Sacramento, California 95819
www.csus.edu

Cary Institute of Ecosystem Studies
2801 Sharon Turnpike
Millbrook, New York 12545
www.ecostudies.org

Chanticleer
786 Church Road
Wayne, Pennsylvania 19087
www.chanticleergarden.org

Chicago Botanic Garden
1000 Lake Cook Road
Glencoe, Illinois 60022
www.chicagobotanic.org

Coastal Maine Botanical Gardens
Barters Island Road
Boothbay, Maine 04537
www.mainegardens.org

Crystal Springs Rhododendron Garden
5801 SE 28th Avenue
Portland, Oregon 97211
www.rhodies.org/xtal/csg_index.htm

Dallas Arboretum and Botanical Garden
8617 Garland Road
Dallas, Texas 75218
www.dallasarboretum.org

Denver Botanic Gardens
1005 York Street
Denver, Colorado 80206
www.botanicgardens.org

Elandan Gardens
3050 W State Highway 16
Bremerton, Washington 98312
www.elandangardens.com

Elisabeth Carey Miller Botanical Garden
P.O. Box 77377
Seattle, Washington 98177
www.millergarden.org

Fairchild Tropical Botanical Garden
10901 Old Cutler Road
Miami, Florida 33156
www.fairchildgarden.org

Fern Canyon
Prairie Creek Redwoods State Park
15336 Highway 101
Trinidad, California 95510
www.parks.ca.gov/?page_id=415

Ferndell Canyon in Griffith Park
5375 Red Oak Drive
Los Angeles, California 90027
www.laparks.org/dos/parks/griffithPK/
ferndell.htm

**Fernwood Botanical Garden and
Nature Preserve**
13988 Range Line Road
Niles, Michigan 49120
www.fernwoodbotanical.org

Fort Worth Botanic Garden
3220 Botanic Garden Blvd.
Fort Worth, Texas 76107
www.fwbg.org

Frelinghuysen Arboretum
353 E Hanover Avenue
Morristown, New Jersey 07960
www.arboretumfriends.org

Garden in the Woods
180 Hemenway Road
Framingham, Massachusetts 01701
www.newenglandwild.org/visit

Garvan Woodland Gardens
550 Arkridge Road
Hot Springs, Arkansas 71913
www.garvangardens.org

Ganna Walska Lotusland
695 Ashley Road
Santa Barbara, California 93108
www.lotusland.org

Georgeson Botanical Garden
University of Alaska
P.O. Box 757200
Fairbanks, Alaska 99775
www.uaf.edu/salrm/gbg

**Georgia Perimeter College
Botanical Gardens**
3251 Panthersville Road
Decatur, Georgia 30016
www.gpc.edu/~decbt/

Harry P. Leu Gardens
1920 N Forest Avenue
Orlando, Florida 32803
www.leugardens.org

Hawaii Tropical Botanical Garden
27-717 Old Mamalahoa Highway
Papaikov, Hawaii 96781
www.htbg.com

Holden Arboretum
9500 Sperry Road
Kirtland, Ohio 44094
www.holdenarb.org

Honolulu Botanical Gardens
50 N Vineyard Blvd.
Honolulu, Hawaii 96817
www.honolulu.gov/parks/hbg.html
*There are five distinct gardens in the system
in different ecological settings around the
island of Oahu.*

Huntington Botanical Gardens
1151 Oxford Road
San Marino, California 91108
www.huntington.org

**Huntsville-Madison County
Botanical Garden**
4747 Bob Wallace Avenue
Huntsville, Alabama 35805
www.hsvbg.org

Inniswood Metro Gardens
940 S Hempstead Road
Westerville, Ohio 43081
www.inniswood.org

Kruckeberg Botanic Garden
20312 15th Avenue NW
Shoreline, Washington 98117
www.kruckeberg.org

Lakewold Gardens
12317 Gravelly Lake Drive SW
Lakewood, Washington 98499
www.lakewoldgardens.org

Leach Botanical Garden
6704 SE 122nd Avenue
Portland, Oregon 97236
www.leachgarden.org

Leonard J. Buck Garden
11 Layton Road
Far Hills, New Jersey 07931
www.somersetcountyparks.org/
parksFacilities/buck/LJBuck.html

Lewis Ginter Botanical Garden
1800 Lakeside Avenue
Richmond, Virginia 23228
www.lewisginter.org

Longwood Gardens
1001 Longwood Road
Kennett Square, Pennsylvania 19348
www.longwoodgardens.org

Lyndhurst Gardens
635 S Broadway
Tarrytown, New York 10591
www.lyndhurst.org

Marie Selby Botanical Gardens
811 South Palm Avenue
Sarasota, Florida 34236
www.selby.org

Matthaei Botanical Gardens
The University of Michigan
1800 N Dixboro Road
Ann Arbor, Michigan 48105
www.lsa.umich.edu/mbg

Memphis Botanic Garden
750 Cherry Road
Memphis, Tennessee 38117
www.memphisbotanicgarden.com

Mendocino Coast Botanical Gardens
18220 North Highway 1
Fort Bragg, California 95437
www.gardenbythesea.org

Mercer Arboretum and Botanic Gardens
22306 Aldine Westfield Road
Humble, Texas 77338
www.hcp4.net/mercer

Michigan State University
W. J. Beal Botanical Garden
West Circle Drive
East Lansing, Michigan 48824
www.cpa.msu.edu/beal

Missouri Botanical Garden
4344 Shaw Blvd.
St. Louis, Missouri 63166
www.missouribotanicalgarden.org

Morris Arboretum of the University of Pennsylvania
100 E Northwestern Avenue
Philadelphia, Pennsylvania 19118
www.morrisarboretum.org

Mount Pisgah Arboretum
34901 Frank Parrish Road
Eugene, Oregon 97405
www.mountpisgaharboretum.org

Mt. Cuba Center
3120 Barley Mill Road
Hockessin, Delaware 19807
www.mtcubacenter.org

National Tropical Botanical Garden
3530 Papalina Road
Kalaheo, Hawaii 96765
www.ntbg.org

New Jersey State Botanical Garden at Skyland
1304 Sloatsburg Road
Ringwood, New Jersey 07456
www.njbg.org

New York Botanical Garden
200th Street and Kazimiroff Blvd.
Bronx, New York 10458
www.nybg.org

Norfolk Botanical Garden
6700 Azalea Garden Road
Norfolk, Virginia 23518
www.norfolkbotanicalgarden.org

North Carolina Botanical Garden
100 Old Mason Farm Road
Chapel Hill, North Carolina 27517
www.ncbg.unc.edu

Olbrich Botanical Garden
3330 Atwood Avenue
Madison, Wisconsin 53704
www.olbrich.org

Phipps Conservatory and Botanical Gardens
One Schenley Park
Pittsburg, Pennsylvania 15213
www.phipps.conservatory.org

Planting Fields Arboretum State Historic Park
1395 Planting Fields Road
Oyster Bay, New York 11771
www.plantingfields.org

Rancho Santa Ana Botanic Garden
1500 North College Avenue
Claremont, California 91711
www.rsabg.org

Rhododendron Species Botanical Garden
2525 S 336th Street
Federal Way, Washington 98003
www.rhodygarden.org

Rotary Gardens
1455 Palmer Drive
Janesville, Wisconsin 53545
www.rotarygardens.org

San Antonio Botanical Garden
555 Funston Place
San Antonio, Texas 78209
www.sabot.org

San Diego Botanic Garden
230 Quail Gardens Drive
Encinitas, California 92023
www.sdbgarden.org

San Francisco Botanical Garden at Strybing Arboretum
Golden Gate Park
9th Avenue at Lincoln Way
San Francisco, California 94122
www.sfbotanicalgarden.org

Sarah P. Duke Gardens
420 Anderson Street
Box 90341
Durham, North Carolina 27708
www.gardens.duke.edu

Tyringham Cobble
Jerusalem Road
Tyringham, Massachusetts 01264
www.thetrustees.org/places-to-visit/
berkshires/tyringham-cobble.html

UNC at Charlotte Botanical Gardens
9201 University City Blvd.
Charlotte, North Carolina 28223
www.gardens.uncc.edu

University of California Botanical Garden at Berkeley
200 Centennial Drive
Berkeley, California 94720
www.botanicalgarden.berkeley.edu

USCS Arboretum
1500 High Street
Santa Cruz, California 95064
arboretum.ucsc.edu

Whitehall Historic Home and Garden
3110 Lexington Road
Louisville, Kentucky 40206
www.historichomes.org/Whitehall/
WelcometoWhitehall/tabid/1444/
Default.aspx

Wild Gardens of Acadia
Acadia National Park
Bar Harbor, Maine 04609
www.nps.gov/acad/planyourvisit/Wild-
Gardens-of-Acadia.htm

Zilker Botanical Garden
2220 Barton Springs Road
Austin, Texas 78746
www.zilkergarden.org

WALES

Aberglasney Gardens
Llangathen
Carmarthenshire SA32 8QH
www.aberglasney.org

Dewstow Gardens
Caerwent
Monmouthshire
South Wales NP26 5AH
www.dewstow.com

Dyffryn Gardens
St. Nicolas
Vale of Glamorgan CF5 6SU
www.dyffryngardens.org.uk

FOR MORE INFORMATION

BOOKS

Cobb, Boughton, Elizabeth Farnsworth, and Cheryl Lowe. 2005. *A Field Guide to Ferns and Their Related Families: Northeastern and Central North America*. Boston: Houghton Mifflin.

Cullina, William. 2008. *Native Ferns, Moss, and Grasses*. Boston: Houghton Mifflin Harcourt.

Dyce, James W., Robert Sykes, and Martin Rickard. 2005. *Polystichum Cultivars: Variations in the British Shield Ferns*. Special Publication No. 7. London: The British Pteridological Society.

Hardy Fern Foundation Quarterly. 1989–2014. Federal Way, Washington.

Hoshizaki, Barbara Joe, and Robbin C. Moran. 2001. *Fern Grower's Manual*. Portland, Oregon: Timber Press.

Jones, David L. 1987. *Encyclopaedia of Ferns*. Portland, Oregon: Timber Press.

Mickel, John T. 1994. *Ferns for American Gardens*. New York: Macmillan.

Olsen, Sue. 2007. *Encyclopedia of Garden Ferns*. Portland, Oregon: Timber Press.

Rickard, Martin. 2000. *The Plantfinder's Guide to Garden Ferns*. Devon, England: David and Charles; Portland, Oregon: Timber Press.

WEBSITES

Hardy Fern Library: www.hardyfernlibrary.com

ORGANIZATIONS

The American Fern Society: www.amerfernsoc.org

The British Pteridological Society: www.eBPS.org.uk

The Hardy Fern Foundation: www.hardyferns.org

HARDINESS ZONE TEMPERATURES

USDA ZONES & CORRESPONDING TEMPERATURES

Temp °F			Zone	Temp °C		
−60	to	−55	1a	−51	to	−48
−55	to	−50	1b	−48	to	−46
−50	to	−45	2a	−46	to	−43
−45	to	−40	2b	−43	to	−40
−40	to	−35	3a	−40	to	−37
−35	to	−30	3b	−37	to	−34
−30	to	−25	4a	−34	to	−32
−25	to	−20	4b	−32	to	−29
−20	to	−15	5a	−29	to	−26
−15	to	−10	5b	−26	to	−23
−10	to	−5	6a	−23	to	−21
−5	to	0	6b	−21	to	−18
0	to	5	7a	−18	to	−15
5	to	10	7b	−15	to	−12
10	to	15	8a	−12	to	−9
15	to	20	8b	−9	to	−7
20	to	25	9a	−7	to	−4
25	to	30	9b	−4	to	−1
30	to	35	10a	−1	to	2
35	to	40	10b	2	to	4
40	to	45	11a	4	to	7
45	to	50	11b	7	to	10
50	to	55	12a	10	to	13
55	to	60	12b	13	to	16
60	to	65	13a	16	to	18
65	to	70	13b	18	to	21

FIND HARDINESS MAPS ON THE INTERNET.

United States *http://www.usna.usda.gov/Hardzone/ushzmap.html*
Canada *http://www.planthardiness.gc.ca/*
Europe *http://www.gardenweb.com/zones/europe/* or *http://www.uk.garden web.com/forums/zones/hze.html*

ACKNOWLEDGMENTS

Many thanks to the many friends including members of the Hardy Fern Foundation and British Pteridological Society who have shared their gardens, enthusiasm, and expertise with us over the years. They have been wonderful visits and we sincerely wish we could include photos from every garden. There is room for some photos however and we would like to recognize with thanks the following hosts: the late Graham Ackers, Pat and Grace Acock, Clive and Doreen Brotherton, Sylvia Duryee, Susan Eggers, Ed and Kathy Fries, Wolfram Gassner, Roger Golding, Yvonne Golding, Dick Hayward, Michael Hayward, Jennifer Ide, Stefan Jessen, Pat Kennar, Andrew Leonard, the late Edward Needham, Roger and Sue Norman, Ernie and Marietta O'Byrne, Plas Brondanw, Tim Pyner, Julian Reed, Martin Rickard, Pat and Walt Riehl, David Schwartz, Bryan and Gill Smith, Tom Stuart, Rolf and Angelika Thiemann, Richard and Diane Treganowan, and Alastair and Jackie Wardlaw.

For outstanding gardens among many, we are happy to include and recommend visits to the following gardens and nurseries: Aberglasney House and Gardens, Bartholomew's Cobble, Bellevue Botanical Garden, Brodsworth Hall and Gardens, Cady Falls Nursery, Caher Bridge Garden, Coastal Maine Botanical Garden, Dallas Arboretum and Botanical Garden, Dewstow Gardens and Hidden Grottoes, Elisabeth C. Miller Botanical Garden, Fibrex Nursery, Georgia Perimeter College Botanical Garden, Gossler Farms, Greencombe Gardens, Hardy Fern Foundation Garden at the Rhododendron Species Botanical Garden, Larnach Castle, Logan Botanic Garden, Ashwood Nurseries, Dig Nursery, Molbak's Garden and Home, Morris Arboretum, Mt. Cuba Center, Plant Delights Nursery, The Fern Nursery, Tatton Park, University of California Botanical Garden at Berkeley, University of North Carolina Garden, and Whitehall Historic Home and Garden. Details can be found in the photo credits, and other gardens of interest can be found in the list of places to see ferns.

In addition, very special thanks go to Michelle Bundy and Loyd Jacobs for their support and to Naud Burnett and Martin Rickard for organizing a number of outstanding tours to exceptional gardens as well as fern-rich sites in the wild. They have been immensely enjoyable and helpful excursions.

We would like to dedicate this work to Sue's children, Greg, Kris, and Tamra Olsen, and to Richie's partner, Rick Peterson, and parents, Jean and Gary Steffen, with our love and thanks.

PHOTO CREDITS

SUE OLSEN, pages 8–9, 20, 37, 42, 55, 62–63, 84 (lower), 86, 90 (upper), 97 (lower), 98, 99 (right), 101 (upper), 102, 104, 109 (right), 113, 115, 118, 125, 129, 136–139, 143 (lower), 146 (upper), 147 (upper), 148 (lower), 151 (upper), 152, 153 (upper), 155 (upper), 156, 157 (upper), 158 (left), 159 (right), 170 (upper right), 173–174, 175 (lower), 178 (lower), 179 (lower left & lower right), 182, 184 (lower), 186 (upper), 188 (left), 189, 191 (upper left & lower left), 192 (left), 193, 197 (left), 198, 201 (right), 202–203, 213, 225.

RICHIE STEFFEN, pages 2–7, 10–19, 21–36, 38–41, 43–53, 54 (left), 56–61, 64–83, 84 (upper), 85, 87–89, 90 (lower), 91–96, 97 (upper right & upper left), 99 (left), 100, 101 (lower), 103, 105–108, 109 (upper left & lower left), 110–112, 114, 116–117, 119–124, 126–128, 130–135, 140–142, 143 (upper), 144–145, 146 (lower left & lower right), 147 (lower), 148 (upper), 149–150, 151 (lower), 153 (lower), 154, 155 (lower), 157 (lower), 158 (right), 159 (left), 160–169, 170 (upper left & lower left), 171–172, 175 (upper), 176–177, 178 (upper), 179 (upper right & center right), 180–181, 183, 184 (upper), 185, 186 (lower), 187, 188 (right), 190, 191 (right), 192 (right), 194–195, 197 (right), 199–200, 201 (left), 204–212, 215–224.

PHOTO LOCATIONS

ABERGLASNEY HOUSE & GARDENS, pages 10–11, 20, 95, 135 (right), 164–165, 170 (upper left).

GRAHAM ACKERS GARDEN, pages 152 (upper), 178 (upper).

PAT ACOCK GARDEN, page 180 (lower).

BARTHOLOMEW'S COBBLE, page 155 (upper).

BELLEVUE BOTANICAL GARDEN, pages 42, 54–55, 62–63, 101 (upper), 102, 157 (upper), 170 (upper right), 179 (lower right), 186 (upper).

BRODSWORTH HALL & GARDENS, pages 40–41, 149 (upper left).

CLIVE & DOREEN BROTHERTON GARDEN, page 113.

CADY FALLS NURSERY (DON & LELA AVERY), page 173 (left).

CAHER BRIDGE, pages 8–9.

CHARLESTON, South Carolina, page 128.

COASTAL MAINE BOTANICAL GARDEN, page 125.

DALLAS ARBORETUM & BOTANICAL GARDEN, pages 29 (lower), 43, 119, 200.

DEWSTOW GARDENS & HIDDEN GROTTOES, pages 24 (upper left), 39, 98 (left).

SYLVIA DURYEE GARDEN, page 159 (right).

SUSAN EGGERS GARDEN, page 96 (lower).

ELISABETH C. MILLER BOTANICAL GARDEN, pages 14–15, 21 (upper & lower), 22 (left), 24 (upper right), 41, 51, 85, 92, 103, 108, 109 (lower left), 124, 127, 140 (upper & lower), 141 (left), 142, 151 (lower), 155 (lower), 159 (left), 160, 161 (right), 169, 191 (right), 207, 209, 210–211, 216.

FIBREX NURSERY, page 175 (upper).

KATHY & ED FRIES GARDEN, pages 24 (lower), 27, 106, 141 (right), 147 (lower), 150, 185, 212.

WOLFRAM GASSNER GARDEN, page 90.

GEORGIA PERIMETER COLLEGE BOTANICAL GARDEN, pages 84 (lower), 114 (left), 205.

ROGER GOLDING GARDEN, pages 144, 172, 178 (lower), 194, 217.

YVONNE GOLDING GARDEN, page 181 (right).

GOSSLER FARMS, pages 52–53.

GREAT SMOKY MOUNTAINS, page 137 (lower).

GREENCOMBE GARDENS, page 195 (left).

HARDY FERN FOUNDATION, pages 16, 19, 34, 109 (upper left), 152 (lower), 153 (upper).

DICK HAYWARD GARDEN, page 162.

MICHAEL HAYWARD GARDEN, pages 97 (right), 177 (lower).

JENNIFER IDE GARDEN, pages 4–5, 17.

STEFAN JESSEN GARDEN, page 203.

PAT KENNAR GARDEN, page 189.

LARNACH CASTLE, page 116.

ANDREW LEONARD GARDEN, page 199.

LOGAN BOTANIC GARDEN, page 104.

JOHN MASSEY (ASHWOOD NURSERIES), pages 48, 64, 167.

MATLOCK & JOHNSON GARDEN (DIG NURSERY), page 206.

MOLBAK'S GARDEN & HOME, page 173 (right).

MORRIS ARBORETUM, pages 196–197.

MT. CUBA CENTER, pages 138 (left), 201 (upper).

EDWARD NEEDHAM GARDEN, page 128.

NEW JERSEY COAST, page 202.

ROGER & SUE NORMAN GARDEN, pages 36–37, 60, 190, 204 (upper).

ERNIE & MARIETTA O'BYRNE GARDEN, pages 6, 18, 28–29, 80, 88, 94, 133, 134–135 (upper), 145, 146 (left), 166.

OLSEN GARDEN, pages 86, 98 (right), 99 (right), 115, 136, 137 (upper), 138 (right), 139, 147 (upper), 148 (lower), 151 (upper), 156 (lower), 158 (left), 174, 179 (left), 184 (lower), 188 (left), 191 (upper left & lower left), 192 (right), 193, 198, 225.

PETERSON & STEFFEN GARDEN, pages 24 (lower right), 32–33, 35, 46, 54 (left), 59, 81, 95, 96 (left & right), 97 (upper left), 100 (upper & lower), 114 (right), 122–123, 143, 153 (lower), 158 (right), 183 (upper & lower), 185 (right), 186 (lower), 197 (right), 204 (lower right), 210–211.

PLANT DELIGHTS NURSERY, pages 82, 90 (lower), 93, 112 (right), 131, 195 (right).

PLAS BRONDANW GARDEN, page 91.

TIM PYNER GARDEN, pages 17, 23, 105 (left), 121, 132, 219.

JULIAN REED GARDEN, page 30.

RHODODENDRON SPECIES BOTANICAL GARDEN, page 156 (upper).

MARTIN RICKARD GARDEN, page 22 (right).

PAT & WALT RIEHL GARDEN, pages 58, 157 (lower), 179 (upper right).

SALZBURG, Austria, page 213.

DAVID SCHWARTZ GARDEN, page 83.

BRYAN & GILL SMITH GARDEN, pages 180 (upper right), 201 (lower left).

TOM STUART GARDEN, page 143 (lower).

INDEX

ABOUT THE AUTHORS

LILLIAN BENNET

YUEN LUI STUDIO

RICHIE STEFFEN is curator of the Elisabeth C. Miller Botanical Garden in Seattle, where he oversees the plant record database, general horticulture, and manages the garden's special collections, including ferns. A well-known personality on the Pacific Northwest horticulture scene, he regularly lectures and writes, and currently serves as a board member of the Northwest Horticultural Society and the Hardy Fern Foundation (past president). He is a superb photographer and is building an archival image collection at Miller Garden.

SUE OLSEN has been studying, photographing, and writing about ferns for more than four decades, and is author of the award-winning *Encyclopedia of Garden Ferns*. Her nursery, Foliage Gardens, has introduced numerous ferns to horticulture and is the oldest mail-order supplier in the United States for spore-grown hardy ferns. A founding member and first president of the Hardy Fern Foundation, Sue is editor of the *Hardy Fern Foundation Quarterly*.

Front cover: *Athyrium otophorum*
Spine: *Polystichum xiphophyllum*
Title page: *Athyrium niponicum* cultivars
Contents page: *Asplenium scolopendrium* Crispum Group

Published in 2015 by Timber Press, Inc.

The Haseltine Building   6a Londsdale Road
133 S.W. Second Avenue, Suite 450   London NW6 6RD
Portland, Oregon 97204-3527

For details on other Timber Press books and to sign up for our newsletters, please visit our websites, timberpress.com and timberpress.co.uk.

Library of Congress Cataloging-in-Publication Data
Steffen, Richie.
  The plant lover's guide to ferns/Richie Steffen and Sue Olsen.—First edition.
     pages cm
  Includes index.
  ISBN 978-1-60469-474-1
  1. Ferns. I. Olsen, Sue (Suzanne) II. Title.
  SB429.S75 2015
  635.9'373—dc23
                         2014032416

A catalog record for this book is also available from the British Library.

Book and cover design by Laken Wright
Printed in China

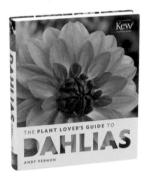

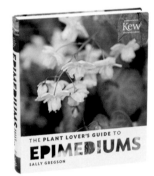